D1414313

LOSING HEARTS AND MINDS?

LOSING HEARTS AND MINDS?

Public Diplomacy and Strategic Influence
in the Age of Terror

Carnes Lord

Foreword by John Hughes

PRAEGER SECURITY INTERNATIONAL
Westport, Connecticut · London

Library of Congress Cataloging-in-Publication Data

Lord, Carnes.
    Losing hearts and minds? : public diplomacy and strategic influence in the
age of terror / Carnes Lord; foreword by John Hughes.
        p. cm.
    Includes bibliographical references and index.
    ISBN 0–275–99082–6 (alk. paper)
    1. United States—Foreign relations—2001– 2. War on Terrorism, 2001– 3. United
States—Foreign relations administration. 4. Bureaucracy—United States. 5. United
States—Strategic aspects. 6. Diplomacy. 7. International relations—Psychological
aspects. 8. Public relations and politics—United States. I. Title.
JZ1480.L67   2006
327.73—dc22   2006015431

British Library Cataloguing in Publication Data is available.

Library of Congress Catalog Card Number: 2006015431
ISBN: 0–275–99082–6

First published in 2006

Praeger Security International, 88 Post Road West, Westport, CT 06881
An imprint of Greenwood Publishing Group, Inc.
www.praeger.com

Printed in the United States of America

The paper used in this book complies with the
Permanent Paper Standard issued by the National
Information Standards Organization (Z39.48–1984).

10 9 8 7 6 5 4 3 2 1

Contents

Foreword

As the Director of the Voice of America in the bad old days of the Cold War, I got the greatest satisfaction in hearing from people living behind the iron curtain. Sometimes they listened to our broadcasts at some peril. One listener crept out in the snow to a stand of birch trees where he surreptitiously tuned in to the Voice of America by short-wave radio. "Your broadcasts," he wrote, "keep the flame of liberty burning in our breasts."

Broadcasting by U.S. government radios—Radio Free Europe and Radio Liberty as well as the Voice of America—played a significant role in fanning the flame of liberty that eventually would free many countries from the grasp of communism. Those broadcasts, in concert with the work of the United States Information Agency (USIA), the parent organization of the Voice of America, is what we call public diplomacy today. Its aim is reaching people around the world with a truthful picture of America to promote democratic values.

Although broadcasting during the Cold War predominantly used short-wave transmitters to reach countries.whose regimes often tried to jam the airwaves, USIA depended on other media to communicate. The agency printed magazines in foreign languages. Under one agreement, for example, periodicals were printed in Russian for distribution in the Soviet Union while a Soviet magazine produced in English was circulated in the United States. Another publication, much in demand among intellectuals, offered serious analysis of communism. In addition, live interviews with American spokesmen were televised abroad for foreign journalists.

Where possible, USIA operated centers abroad to distribute books, magazines, and films about America. The centers were staffed by seasoned public affairs officers who cultivated local columnists, editors, and broadcasters to foster a dialogue on international affairs and U.S. foreign policy. The officers were not only posted to the capitals of unfriendly nations, but to cities such as London, Paris, and Rome to reach audiences in important allied nations.

Other USIA programs included exchanges with journalists, politicians, jurists, scientists, and other professionals. Selected foreign nationals were invited to the United States for contacts with their counterparts and exposure to the American way of life. Similarly, our citizens went abroad to talk about America. In addition, ambitious cultural exchanges enabled U.S. orchestras, choirs, and dance companies to visit many countries, usually with a rapturous response.

With the end of the Cold War and the relaxation of international tension, the apparatus of public diplomacy began to be cut back. Funding for various programs dried up. Finally, USIA was dismembered and merged into the Department of State. The cheerful thesis advanced was that our enemies had been vanquished and thus the need for public diplomacy had waned.

But as Carnes Lord—a former White House official who has been intimately involved in public diplomacy—makes clear in *Losing Hearts and Minds?*, that decision was extremely short sighted. Today we are engaged in a war against terrorists who use violent means to kill or maim their victims and who manipulate the internet, television, and other media to rally supporters and misrepresent the United States. President George Bush has warned, since 9/11, that the campaign to root out and neutralize terrorism will be long. An even longer campaign will be waged for the hearts and minds of the next generation of potential terrorists, namely youth being brain-washed about America in fundamentalist *madrasahs*.

We must revitalize public diplomacy to offset hate-laden distortions and bitter resentment with a vision of freedom and the truth about U.S. policy. Carnes Lord has outlined our options and makes recommendations that some readers will find controversial. The overarching value of his book, however, is that it may trigger a meaningful debate on the problems confronting public diplomacy and encourage seizing the available opportunities to overcome them.

John Hughes
Editor and chief operating officer, *Deseret Morning News*,
Salt Lake City and former editor of *The Christian Science Monitor*.
Director of the Voice of America and Assistant Secretary of State for
Public Affairs during the Reagan administration.

Preface

When I first came to have personal experience of the matters discussed in this book, the U.S. government was using radio transmitters that in some cases had seen service in World War II, and electric typewriters were thought to be high technology. A quarter of a century later, globally available television, the computer, and the internet have revolutionized international communications. And yet the problems the United States has encountered in communicating effectively with foreign publics have in fact changed little since 1981—for that matter, since 1941. This study therefore will pay relatively scant attention to recent trends in the global information environment. It concentrates instead on the conceptual, cultural, political, and organizational dimension of American overseas communications policies and activities. To put it graphically but I think accurately, the overseas communications programs of the U.S. government have always been, and remain today, a bureaucratic backwater and cultural tar baby. Unless and until this is recognized and its causes understood, and steps taken to counter it, the most sophisticated technologies will avail us little in conveying America's story to the world.

I owe many debts in connection with this project, and not least, to those currently employed in various agencies of the U.S. government who gave generously of their time and who for the most part, and for obvious reasons, will have to remain anonymous. I am particularly grateful to Christopher Lamb and Jeffrey Jones for an illuminating discussion of current Department of Defense issues, to Stephanie Kinney for help on State Department issues, and to Ambassador

Diana Dougan for pointing the way on White House reorganization. John Hughes has been a source of wisdom for many years on public diplomacy issues in the State Department and USIA. Seth Cropsey provided a key insider's view of the Broadcasting Board of Governors. Kenneth Jensen and Robert Schadler contributed some important insights, as did Sophia Aguirre from the vantage point of the United States Advisory Commission on Public Diplomacy. To Roy Godson and the Bradley Foundation and to Patrick Cronin of the Center for Strategic and International Studies I owe thanks for inviting me to take part in stimulating meetings on this subject. I would also like to make special acknowledgment of the collaboration and support provided by John Lenczowski and Michael Waller of the Institute of World Politics in Washington, D.C., one of the few academic institutions in the country that has given public diplomacy and related disciplines a place of honor in its curriculum. Another is the Naval Postgraduate School, where I owe thanks to Gordon McCormick, Hy Rothstein, and John Arquilla for their hospitality on several occasions, as well as for sponsoring publication of an essay drawing on an earlier draft of some of this material. In addition to that paper, the study also makes use of several other of my earlier publications on this subject: "Psychological–Political Instruments," in Audrey Kurth Cronin and James M. Ludes, eds., *Attacking Terrorism: Elements of a Grand Strategy* (Washington, D.C.: Georgetown University Press, 2003), pp. 220–37, and "Public Diplomacy: Past and Future," *Orbis* (Winter 1998): 433–50. I am grateful for permission to utilize this material. It should go without saying that the views expressed in this study are my own, and are in no way endorsed by the Naval War College or the Department of Defense.

Nadia Schadlow of the Smith Richardson Foundation planted the idea of this project, and I am grateful to the Foundation for their generous support of it. My literary agent Donald Gastwirth has been a faithful adviser and friend. Robert Silano helped arrange publication of this book with Praeger and has encouraged my work in this field in other incarnations. Finally, thanks are due my wife Meredith for acting as an always reliable sounding board and for her loving support; and we both thank the (now sadly departed) United States Information Agency for arranging for us to meet. This book is dedicated to her.

Newport, Rhode Island

CHAPTER 1

Introduction

In the endgame of the Cold War, improving the overseas communications capabilities of the United States was a central component of the Reagan administration's overall strategy for confronting the global Soviet challenge. An important part of this strategy involved—for the first time—a clear national commitment not only to hasten the end of the Communist experiment but to engage America and Americans actively in the promotion of democratic governance throughout the world. This was a commitment which took the form not only of words but of deeds—deeds such as material support for democratic forces in Eastern Europe, which contributed significantly to loosening the Soviet grip on its empire and to its eventual spectacular fall. In retrospect, though, it is clear that Washington's words also had important effects. President Reagan himself understood the potential of "public diplomacy"—this was the term most commonly used by the end of the 1970s to describe the overseas communications activities of governments; and he used the bully pulpit of the White House to let it be known that the Soviet's "empire" was indeed "evil" and would end, quite contrary to its own claim, on the wrong side of history. Following the president's lead, his administration oversaw a revitalization of American public diplomacy programs and assets, especially in the arena of international radio broadcasting, which arguably played a major if still poorly understood role in undermining the Soviet system in its final days.

With the fall of the Berlin Wall, the dismemberment of the Warsaw Pact, and the collapse of the Soviet Union itself, many in Washington felt that America's venerable public diplomacy machinery had outlived its mission. The 1990s saw consistently stagnant or declining budgets for the United States Information Agency (USIA), the primary institutional home of American public diplomacy, as well as the various U.S. international broadcasting organizations. So-called "surrogate broadcasting" to Eastern Europe came under particular pressure, as three services (the Polish, Czech, and Hungarian) of Radio Free Europe/Radio Liberty (RFE-RL) were soon abolished and others reduced sharply. Eventually, in a major if little-noted bureaucratic reorganization in 1999, USIA was formally abolished. While some of its functions and personnel were absorbed by the State Department, it soon became evident that state was far from wholly committed to the public diplomacy mission, and significant capabilities were eroded or lost both in Washington and the field. Moreover, White House (above all, presidential) involvement in public diplomacy, which had reached a postwar peak under Reagan, declined markedly under George H. W. Bush and virtually disappeared in the Clinton years.

It could be argued that these developments were a not wholly unreasonable response to the benign security environment of the immediate post-Cold War era. In the absence of a clear foreign threat or indeed of any coherent ideological opposition to the United States as the recognized hegemon of a "new world order," what exactly was it that public diplomacy needed to say or to do? A celebrated article of this period maintained that what the world was witnessing was nothing less than the "end of history," in the sense of the final resolution of the long-standing conflict between liberal democracy and the non-liberal alternatives to it.[1] The ascendancy of the United States in the world appeared in this light as a necessary and natural consequence of larger historical forces. To the extent that this was really the case, the active promotion of liberal democracy or the image of the nation abroad by the U.S. government would have to be seen as a colossal waste of effort.

The terrorist attacks on New York and Washington on September 11, 2001, ushered in a new era. The sudden emergence of a new military and ideological challenge to the United States and its allies in the form of Islamist terrorism, though hardly of the scale or potentially world-ending seriousness of the Soviet threat, was in some respects more worrisome. For the first time, international terrorism attained "global reach" and capabilities for mass destruction. For the first time also, terrorist tactics were placed in the service of an ideology and political strategy of truly transnational scope, one rooted in a radical or fundamentalist Islam that was rapidly taking hold across the Muslim world. In all of these respects, the new terrorism represented a threat of an order of magnitude greater than traditional forms of terrorism. In fact, it had more in common with the threat posed by Soviet communism (at any rate during its ideologically vigorous period) than with that of traditional, nationally oriented terrorist movements. But it was even more dangerous in some ways. The Soviet Union, for all its unyielding hostility to the West, was a prudent player on the international scene, and could be deterred from using its formidable military power by the countervailing arsenals of the advanced democracies. The soldiers of Al Qaeda, by contrast, gloried in their acts of martyrdom against the "far enemy."

The "global war on terror," as it is now regularly called, is in its fifth year—longer than the period the United States fought in World War II. During this period, the United States and its allies have launched major military campaigns against two countries in the Middle East, conducted military operations or missions in dozens of other countries and on the seas, and carried out extensive intelligence and law enforcement activities targeting Islamist terrorism across the globe. Yet no end to this conflict is now in sight, and there is every reason to suppose it could persist in some form for decades to come. Some have questioned whether the invasion and occupation of Iraq by an American-led coalition in the spring of 2003 can legitimately be considered part of the "war on terror." Whatever the connection between the regime of Saddam Hussein and Al Qaeda or other terrorist organizations, though, and however flawed the rationale for the invasion may have been, there can be little question that the second Iraq war and its aftermath have merged seamlessly into a larger global struggle that can still plausibly be described as the war on terror. Having said this, it is necessary to acknowledge that the war on terror can neither be understood nor effectively waged unless it is seen to be about more than terrorism. The war on terror is no longer, if it ever was, simply about eliminating the Al Qaeda organization and its leadership—those responsible for the assault on America in 9/11. It is rather about something much larger: the shape of the greater Middle East and the future of Islam.

In fact, it is possible to argue that for most practical purposes, Al Qaeda has already been defeated. Many of its senior leaders have been killed or captured, and there is little reason to believe that Osama bin Laden, its nominal chief, retains any operational control over its cadres, though (as of May 2006) he is apparently still alive. If Al Qaeda exists today, it is as a "virtual" organization that lives largely in the minds of men (and courtesy of the internet). At the same time, it has become only too clear in the course of the last several years that Islamist terrorism as inspired by this "virtual" Al Qaeda remains a formidable foe—ruthless, resilient, protean, and impossible to defeat by conventional military methods, at least at a cost acceptable to the United States and world opinion. In the language of strategic analysis, the "center of gravity" of Islamist terrorism lies not in its organizational structure but in its ideological inspiration—the real source of the fresh recruits who continue to flock to the terrorist banner. And its ideological inspiration is primarily a function of the politics and history, not of Islam simply, but of the modern (and primarily Arab) Middle East. Final victory over Islamist terrorism, therefore, seems to call for nothing less than a reshaping if not a transformation of the political and cultural landscape of the Middle East, emphatically including an ideological cleansing of Islam itself. But such a project cannot be achieved by force alone, though force—especially in its application against the regime of Saddam Hussein in Iraq—may well prove to have been an indispensable precondition for it. Rather, it requires a capability for the comprehensive projection of American strategic influence in the region—and beyond.

The administration of George W. Bush has by no means been unmindful of the role of perceptions, opinions, and ideas in the unfolding war on terror, or of the need for the United States to take an active role in molding them. Over the last year, Defense Department documents have explicitly identified "countering ideological support for terrorism" as a key pillar in its counterterrorist strategy. As early as the fall of 2001, the Pentagon recognized the importance of what it called "strategic influence" for the war on terror, and established a new office of that name to carry out an aggressive program of this sort—one that would include but also extend beyond activities generally labeled as public diplomacy. The State Department early on launched a campaign to portray in a favorable light the treatment of Muslim immigrants in the United States and more generally improve America's image, and has continued to pursue efforts at what it calls "Muslim Global Outreach" as part of its new public diplomacy mandate. New and innovative radio and television entities were created to broadcast to the Arab world. In 2002, the White House created a new Office of Global Communications that brought a measure of improved coordination to the U.S. government response to media coverage of the terror war.

Yet in spite of all this, it is universally acknowledged today that the Bush administration has largely failed to craft an effective strategy for projecting global influence in the terror war, or to develop the mechanisms necessary for carrying one out. Interagency cooperation in the public diplomacy arena, rarely smooth, suffered debilitating setbacks as a result of the open warfare between the Departments of Defense and State that complicated U.S. policy toward Iraq, and was never effectively managed by the White House. The Pentagon's Office of Strategic Influence met an ignominious end only months after its creation when internal bureaucratic intrigues spilled over into the national media. At the State Department, public diplomacy was hampered both by persisting institutional weaknesses and by a lack of leadership and imagination at the top. The White House communications operation failed to live up to its initial promise, degenerating into little more than a public relations exercise. Finally, little interest seemed to be shown by senior administration officials in the public diplomacy instrument, including the president himself. This cumulative neglect, coupled with occasional spectacular gaffes (most notably, perhaps, the president's use of the term "crusade" in the context of the terror war, and Defense Secretary Donald Rumsfeld's vocal criticisms of "old" Europe), has arguably contributed in a major way to a near-calamitous decline in the image and reputation of the United States around the world over the last several years.

The lamentable condition of American public diplomacy today is not in dispute. A raft of studies and reports over the last several years by a variety of official, semi-official, and independent bodies from across the political spectrum has told a broadly similar story of institutional ineffectiveness, lack of strategic direction, and insufficient resources.[2] In the aftermath of 9/11, our elected leadership summoned the political will to make the most far-reaching changes in the national security bureaucracy in more than half a century when it created the Department of Homeland Security. At the present time, a similar national commitment to institutional change seems to have emerged in the area of intelligence. Such a commitment does not exist, unfortunately, in the area of public diplomacy and related disciplines. At her Senate confirmation hearings in early 2005, Secretary of State

Condoleezza Rice pledged to make reform of public diplomacy a "top priority," and the appointment of former Bush White House adviser Karen Hughes as under secretary of State for Public Diplomacy and Public Affairs (effective in September 2005) suggested a wider commitment by the administration to address the problem. As yet, however, few concrete signs of real change have emerged.

There are a number of reasons for the difficulty of reform in this arena, but two are critical. Not only is there no real consensus among practitioners or critics of American public diplomacy as to what needs to be done to fix it (apart perhaps from spending more money), but the nature of the pathologies afflicting it are themselves not well understood. The purpose of this study is to provide both a diagnosis of the disease and a comprehensive set of remedial measures.

What accounts for the present condition of American public diplomacy? It is easy enough to blame the end of the Cold War, and the widespread sense it brought that the tides of history were flowing in our direction and that the United States therefore needed to do little to explain itself in a world in which liberalism and democracy were suddenly the norm. In fact, however, the problems facing public diplomacy today have much deeper roots. Even at the height of the Cold War, or for that matter during the Reagan interlude, public diplomacy never fully lived up to the initial expectations held out for it by many, and it remained for the most part at the margins of American grand strategy.[3] Public diplomacy is unique as an instrument of American statecraft. At any rate since the demise of the United States Information Agency, it alone among the elements of our national security policy lacks a core institutional base, an established infrastructure of education and training, a stable cadre of personnel, an operational doctrine, or roles and missions that are understood and accepted by national security professionals and political elites, or for that matter the general public. Not coincidentally, it lacks high-level political support and tends to be chronically under-funded.

Further, public diplomacy operates in a uniquely challenging domestic environment—one centrally shaped by the fundamental hostility of the commercial media and much of the general culture in the United States to any government involvement in the management of information. This environment is reflected in the perennial micromanagement of public diplomacy programs by the Congress, as well as in the bureaucratic culture of most public diplomacy organizations, heavily populated as they are by journalists or those who identify strongly with the journalism profession. Public diplomacy is necessarily in the position of competing with the commercial media, and tends to measure itself according to standards prevailing there. This imperative in turn creates tensions with policy officials within the government, and at the extreme makes it necessary to raise the question of whether this is a business the government should really be in at all. This question seems increasingly legitimate in an era of rapidly expanding global communications and increasing openness, in most societies, to multiple sources of information.

A perennial stumbling block in addressing these issues—and one that continues to have serious practical consequences—is identifying in a generally acceptable manner just what it is we are talking about. The term "public diplomacy," as indicated earlier, is of relatively recent coinage (it dates from the early 1970s), designed essentially to distance American practice from the increasingly pejorative flavor of the term "propaganda." Because there is no official accepted doctrine governing public diplomacy operations, the term has been used in a variety of ways, including, it should be noted, in a domestic context. It coexists uneasily with other, similarly vague terms such as "international information" or "international communication." Toward the harder edge of the spectrum, it competes with terms such as "psychological operations," "psychological warfare," and "political warfare." Very recently, the term "strategic communication" has gained traction within the Department of Defense as an umbrella label embracing public affairs, public diplomacy, and military psychological operations ("PSYOP"). Confusingly, however, psychological operations also figures as a component of the new military discipline known as "information operations." Finally, there is the term "strategic influence," also doctrinally undefined, and now out of favor within the Pentagon.[4]

It is a serious mistake to consider all this merely a matter of semantics. Different terms have very distinct histories and—the critical point—embody different bureaucratic equities. Failure to develop an agreed vocabulary for speaking of these issues therefore contributes directly to organizational lack of coordination and general dysfunction. The next two chapters will address questions relating to the definition and scope both of the larger policy arena in play here and the particular disciplines that populate it. To avoid misunderstanding, let it be stated at the outset that I use "public diplomacy" in a relatively robust sense that covers information across a broad spectrum (from near-term policy-related to long-term generic), cultural affairs, and what I will call "political action." Public diplomacy so understood is primarily a function of today's State Department and international broadcasting organizations. It is one part of a more general complex of disciplines that I prefer to call "psychological-political warfare," though that term has no standing currently within the U.S. government, which spans the defense and intelligence establishments. Finally, I use "strategic influence" as a still more comprehensive term that combines psychological-political warfare with elements of diplomacy and international assistance. It is essentially synonymous with the term "soft power" coined recently by the political scientist Joseph Nye, a term that has achieved wide currency (though, again, no official status). As will become apparent, I find the term useful if only to underline the essential unity—and increasing interdependence—of a variety of bureaucratic disciplines that in the past have too often had little to do with one another, when not actively engaging in guerrilla warfare over turf or resources.

After reviewing the tangle of conceptual and definitional questions raised by public diplomacy and strategic influence and how they have played out in the recent history of these disciplines, I provide (in Chapter 4) an overview of their place in the contemporary security environment and the role they should properly play in American strategy and statecraft. This discussion focuses primarily on the war on terror in its various dimensions, but it also goes beyond it to address the indispensable (yet today almost totally neglected) question of how public diplomacy and strategic influence can help define, shape, and project the image of the United States and its people. This question is less about "selling" America—though the techniques of Madison Avenue are not necessarily always to be despised—than it is about articulating a detailed and substantive vision of what America is and what its proper role should be in the world of the 21st century. At least some of the anti-Americanism that is rampant in the world today, contrary to some alarmist analyses, is probably transitory, a function of the daily media diet of stories and images from the terror war. On the other hand, much of it is certainly real and relatively deepseated, and not all of that is without some measure of justification in our nation's policies and actions and how we explain them—or fail to do so. A genuinely serious public diplomacy needs, for example, a well-thought-out position on the issue of whether or to what extent America's emerging world role is an "imperial" one in any sense. As I shall argue, there has been a great deal of very loose talk in academic and policy circles in the United States on this theme, almost certainly with very adverse consequences for perceptions of the United States by friends and foes alike. American public diplomatists should be able to explain in a careful and compelling way (which is not to say that they will always convince) why the United States, some appearances to the contrary notwithstanding, is not and will not become an empire. At the same time, it may also be the case that the United States needs to make some adjustments in its policies or its actual actions in order to lend credibility and strength to these arguments. One of the themes of this book is the importance of closer integration between public diplomacy or strategic influence operations and policy writ large (and with diplomatic operations).

In the chapters that follow (Chapters 5 and 6), I will then analyze the two principal factors underlying the congenital weaknesses in contemporary American public diplomacy, going back to its formative period in World War II and the early Cold War. These are, first, the lack of legitimacy of government-sponsored information or influence programs in the context of American political culture, and second, the inherent difficulty of organizing the government effectively to plan and carry out such programs. Chapter 5 focuses especially on the problematic relationship between public diplomacy and commercial journalism, but also broaches the sensitive (indeed, generally unmentionable) subject of the extent to which public diplomacy today is inhibited by the culture of "political correctness" emanating from contemporary American liberalism as well as the partisan agendas that it seeks to advance. This is reflected in its most concrete form in the extraordinary history of congressional micromanagement of public diplomacy programs alluded to earlier.

The general discussion and historical overview of the evolution of the organization of the U.S. government for public diplomacy in Chapter 6 creates a framework for the detailed analysis of the American national security bureaucracy that is developed in the following four chapters. In Chapter 7, the discussion centers on the question of whether the current organization of the Department of State is adequate for the public diplomacy mission, and if not, whether there are any satisfactory fixes short of reconstituting the old USIA or something resembling it—that is, an agency whose sole mission would be to keep alight the public diplomacy flame. I try to make the case that, short of a fundamental transformation of the bureaucratic culture of the State Department, a revived USIA is an essential element in any serious reform of American public diplomacy. I also suggest changes that would have the effect of better integrating public diplomacy at the State Department with a wider array of influence operations (particularly in the area of democracy promotion and human rights) as well as with diplomacy as such.

Chapter 8 traces the largely unheralded but substantial changes that have occurred in the organization and direction of the U.S. government's international broadcasting establishment during and since the Cold War. It makes the case that the current organizational arrangement, under which all U.S. broadcasting entities are subordinated to a Broadcasting Board of Governors (BBG) made up of private citizens appointed by the president, has become thoroughly dysfunctional and requires sweeping reform. Instead of the BBG, which in practice is accountable to no one, a reconstituted USIA should be given (for the first time) oversight responsibilities for all U.S. international broadcasters, which should be consolidated in a single new operating entity. Apart from these narrow organizational matters, I also make some suggestions for reforming the culture and command relationships of these organizations so as to clarify the rights and responsibilities of the U.S. government in the management of "news"—a perennially neuralgic issue in the public diplomacy world. I believe it is essential to develop a new model of official broadcasting to meet the requirements both of evolving communications technologies and of the lethal strategic environment in which we now find ourselves.

My discussion of the Department of Defense in Chapter 9 further develops the theme that public diplomacy and strategic influence today need to be broadly rethought in the context of the protracted if mostly low-level global war in which we are now engaged. For the most part, little attention has been paid in the past by practitioners of traditional public diplomacy or in the literature on this subject to the existing role or potential future contributions of the Pentagon in this arena. Within the Department of Defense (DoD), information-related functions and personnel—principally, public affairs and military psychological operations—have historically been lightly regarded, had very limited horizons, and have been virtually incapable of operating effectively in an interagency setting. After 9/11, the evident failure of the State Department to mount effective public diplomacy operations in support of the terror war led DoD to increase its own involvement—in the first instance, as discussed earlier, through the creation of an Office of Strategic Influence. After the occupation of Iraq, the Pentagon was faced with massive requirements in the theater of operations for what has come to be called "strategic communication." It was largely unprepared for these, and its performance left a great deal to be desired. Currently, progress in developing such capabilities is being hindered by ongoing disputes within DoD over the scope of the strategic communication function and the proper relationship between its public affairs and PSYOP components, as well as by continuing uncertainty as to a possible DoD role in the area of "public diplomacy" proper. I suggest some possible solutions to these problems, including a redefinition of the PSYOP function and recognition of a distinctive discipline of defense-related public diplomacy staffed by military and civilian DoD personnel in new dedicated organizations in both Washington and the field.

The well-documented inadequacies of the individual government agencies active in this field as well as the lack of effective coordination among them[5] has led many to the view that the White House is the real answer in any approach to reforming our current arrangements. Chapter 10 reviews the history of White House and presidential involvement in public diplomacy and various current proposals for strengthening centralized management of the interagency process in this area. While some measure of improved central planning and direction for public diplomacy is certainly needed, I argue that centralized public diplomacy operations are difficult if not impossible to manage in a timely and effective manner, and that the key to reform is rather a strengthening of institutional capacities and reform of operational cultures in the relevant agencies. However, it is also important to keep in view the critical operational role played in public diplomacy—for good or for ill—by the president's own speeches and actions.

As everyone knows, there have been far-reaching changes in the technologies of international communications over the past several decades. The internet in particular has vastly increased the access of peoples throughout the world to information that may be unwelcome to their own governments, and is therefore both a conduit and a competitor for official government public diplomacy efforts. The same can be said to some degree of satellite-based radio and television, especially in the strategically vital Middle East. Almost certainly, the net effects of these developments are as yet not well understood, and the emerging possibilities not yet fully grasped or exploited by the governments that have been active in public diplomacy. While these developments will not be ignored in this study, however, they will not be discussed in detail.[6] The reasons for this should by now be evident. The real problems that continue to hobble the performance of American public diplomacy are not primarily technical problems, but problems of organization and culture.

For those who have not worked in government, it is easy to underestimate the impact of organizational factors on performance.

As President Dwight D. Eisenhower classically put it:

Organization cannot make a genius out of an incompetent; even less can it, of itself, make the decisions which are required to trigger the necessary action. On the other hand, disorganization can scarcely fail to result in inefficiency and can easily lead to disaster.[7]

The same is true with cultural factors, if not indeed more so as they tend to be less visible. Within government, it is common enough to hear the refrain that all that matters is hiring the right people. While there is certainly something to this, it is far from the whole story. Criteria of selection of "the right people" are themselves shaped by cultural predispositions; moreover, truly talented people can be especially dysfunctional if situated in the wrong box on the organizational chart or assigned unsuitable projects. Much of what I will have to say in this study may seem to have the effect of disparaging the civil servants and appointed leaders who have populated and run the public diplomacy agencies of the U.S. government over the years. This has not been the intention. I know from my own experience that a good many of these people have brought and continue to bring considerable talents and energy to the challenges they face. But they can only do so much, and the odds against success are considerable.

Having said all this, there is a still more fundamental problem that must be taken into account as we seek to understand the pathologies of our subject. It is that many simply do not believe in the value of public diplomacy. Ironically, in view of the pioneering role Americans have had in developing the fields of advertising and public relations, not to speak of religious evangelism, there is today little real understanding either throughout the government or in the intellectual or public policy worlds of the efficacy of words, images, and ideas as instruments of national policy. Too often, public diplomacy is simply dismissed as mere flacking, on the assumption that its target audiences will regard it the same way and be unmoved if not actively alienated by it. It is striking, for example, to what extent the role of American public diplomacy in the winning of the Cold War has been ignored or disparaged. Uncovering the historical roots of this phenomenon is beyond the scope of this study.[8] Nor shall I attempt to address the notoriously elusive question of the metrics of public diplomacy performance. I limit myself here to appealing to the experience and common sense of Americans as they observe the immediate impacts of psychological-political warfare as it is waged by their own politicians in their own newspapers and on their own airwaves.[9] In the next chapter, I will respond at greater length to this skepticism concerning public diplomacy's worth.

A final point may be added. Like it or not, the United States today is at war, and may remain so for years to come. It is understandable that most Americans want to go about their own lives as much as possible without reference to this fact. It is a wholly different matter when politicians and bureaucrats seek to do the same out of political or professional self-interest. Nations unwilling to face the realities of war and to innovate as required to fight them effectively risk unpleasant consequences. Of the instruments of American statecraft, as noted earlier, homeland security and intelligence have been revealed in and by our current war to be seriously defective, and a political consensus has accordingly emerged to push for radical reforms in both realms. It is time to recognize that public diplomacy and strategic influence are similarly broken, and for our political leaders to begin to address how to fix them. Particularly in the kind of war we are engaged in, these instruments could well prove to make the difference between victory and defeat.

CHAPTER 2

Strategic Influence and Soft Power

A major factor contributing to the relative neglect of the study and practice of public diplomacy in the United States and elsewhere is the tendency to view it through the prism of the small and often under-funded and otherwise marginalized government agencies that are responsible for it. From this point of view, it is seen as the last and least of the various instruments of national power. Yet this reflects a fundamental misapprehension. Public diplomacy derives much of its efficacy from the fact that it forms part of a larger whole. This larger whole encompasses not only public words but public deeds—that is to say, government policies and actions. What is more, it extends beyond the operations of government altogether, to the activities of the private sector and to the larger society and culture. A great deal of the work of public diplomacy agencies consists in mobilizing and deploying private sector resources. Public diplomacy is enabled and its effect enhanced by the larger society and culture. At the same time, public diplomacy helps to amplify and advertise that society and culture to the world at large.

"Soft power," a concept popularized in recent years by the political scientist Joseph Nye, is useful for understanding the larger context in which public diplomacy functions.[1] Soft power has been a strong suit for the United States virtually from its inception—certainly long before the country became a recognized world power in the 20th century. American "exceptionalism"—the nation's devotion to freedom, the rule of law, and republican government, its openness to immigrants of all races and religions, its opposition to traditional power politics, and imperialism—has had a great deal to do with the rise of the United States to its currently dominant global role. But other great powers throughout history have also been adept at exploiting the advantages of soft power. The Roman and British empires, for example, were both able to control vast territories with very limited military forces through the appeal of the civilization they spread before them and the relatively benign character of their rule.[2] Today, there are signs that a number of countries besides the United States are becoming more conscious of their own soft power resources and seeking more actively to take advantage of them. Perhaps the best example is the People's Republic of China, which has undertaken a major effort over the last few years to improve its image as a responsible member of the international community and to promote Chinese culture and Chinese language instruction around the world. But comparable developments have been taking place as well in the United Kingdom, France, Germany, and Russia, not to speak of minor states such as Norway or Venezuela or indeed of terrorist organizations like Al Qaeda.

At the same time, voices both at home and abroad have expressed concern that the United States, with its increasing reliance on unilaterally exercised military power, is in danger of forgetting the lessons of its own past by failing to safeguard its soft power resources. Such critics call attention not only to the current low standing of the United States in public opinion in many parts of the world, particularly following its invasion of Iraq, but more fundamentally, the apparent insensitivity of the U.S. government to foreign perceptions of a range of current American policies—domestic (such as adhering to the death penalty) as well as international. In particular, the United States stands accused of failing to take sufficient account of the views and interests of its traditional allies and of international institutions such as the United Nations. The result, it is argued, is what might be described as a crisis of legitimacy in the exercise of American power and the American global role generally.[3]

Let us now look more closely at the nature of soft power and its relationship to the other instruments of national power, taking as our point of departure Nye's extended analysis in his most recent book *Soft Power* (2004).[4] We will then be in a position to assess the relationship between public diplomacy and soft power in the contemporary context of the global war on terror and the United States' new quasi-imperial role in the Middle East.

Nye begins by rightly stressing the elusive nature of the term "power" itself. Many people identify the exercise of power with command or coercion, but questions immediately arise about the motivation of those on the receiving end. Identifying power with measurable resources such as a large population and territory over-looks the importance of the intangibles of leadership and strategy in deploying such resources effectively. Soft power underlines the importance of the intangible dimension of power. Hard power is preeminently military or economic power, operating through threats ("sticks") or inducements ("carrots"). But "a country may obtain the outcomes it wants in world politics because other countries—admiring its values, emulating its example, aspiring to its level of prosperity and openness—want to follow it. In this sense, it is also important to set the agenda and attract others in world politics, and not only to force them to change by threatening military force or economic sanctions. This soft power—getting others to want the outcomes that you want—co-opts people rather than coerces them."[5]

Soft power is not the same as influence, since men are influenced by hard power as much as they are by soft power; nor is it the same as persuasion through argument. "Simply put, soft power is attractive power." This could seem to suggest that soft power is purely passive in its mode of operation, but Nye hastens to correct this impression. Soft power can also rest on "the ability to manipulate the agenda of political choices in a manner that makes others fail to express some preferences because they seem to be too unrealistic." Nye does not give a great deal of emphasis to this agenda-setting aspect of soft power, or for that matter any illustration of it; and his use of the term "manipulation" in this context conjures up a picture somewhat at odds with the notion of soft power as attraction.[6] What he seems to have in mind is the ability of the United States in particular to shape the agenda of world politics through projecting an image of societal success and responsible international leadership.

What are the sources of soft power? Nye identifies three broad categories: "culture," "political values," and "policies." Culture includes high culture and popular culture; both can have potent effects, but the appeal of American popular culture throughout the world probably puts it in a category of its own. The United States also enjoys valuable advantages in terms of political values, as the world's oldest constitutional democracy and an impressive (if far from perfect) showcase of good governance and the rule of law. Finally, the policies of governments, both domestically and abroad, are an obvious source of soft power. America's early commitment to religious toleration, for example, was a powerful element of its overall appeal to potential immigrants, and American aid in the reconstruction of Europe after World War II was an advertisement both of the prosperity and the generosity of the people of the United States.

By the same token, a nation's soft power can be undermined by these same factors. American popular culture is feared and resented in places like France and Saudi Arabia, and acts at cross purposes with government policies that seek to cultivate traditionalist allies in the Islamic world, for example. At home, American soft power has variously been tarnished by policies such as racial segregation, the death penalty, and lax gun control; abroad, recent American policies toward the global environment, the World Court, and the Arab-Israeli dispute, among others, are widely said to have fostered a damaging image of reckless American "unilateralism"—a charge echoed by Nye throughout his book.

Much of what Nye has to say about soft power is unexceptionable, yet his analysis also has its limitations. It can be argued that in spite of his comments on the importance of culture and other societal forces not under the control of governments, Nye in the end significantly understates the contribution of these forces to national power; and this is true above all in the case of the United States. In their outstanding study *America's Inadvertent Empire* (2004), William E. Odom and Robert Dujarric provide a more satisfying account of what they call "the sources of American power," emphasizing in particular the impact abroad of American science and technology, higher education, and media.[7] It is striking that opinion polling in different regions of the world suggests that America is most admired for its scientific and technical achievements.[8] Also striking and little understood is the extent to which American higher education and American scholarship outclass and dominate that of the rest of the world, while the United States continues to be a magnet for foreign students and is able in this way to exert immense influence over the rising generation of intellectual and political elites throughout the world. Finally, American commercial media have penetrated foreign markets to a perhaps surprising extent.[9] Moreover, an aggregate effect of all these developments is to further cement the role of English as the dominant global language.

A second issue concerns the relationship between soft and hard power. Nye admits that this relationship is a complex one.

Hard and soft power sometimes reinforce and sometimes interfere with each other. A country that courts popularity may be loath to exercise its hard power when it should, but a country that throws its weight around without regard to its effects on its soft power may find others placing obstacles in the way of its hard power. No country likes to feel manipulated, even by soft power. At the same time..., hard power can create myths of invincibility or inevitability that attract others.[10]

But it is not clear whether Nye has thought through sufficiently the ways in which hard power may be said to function like soft power—that is, to cast an aura of attraction.

This is especially true in the economic area, where it becomes especially difficult to distinguish between compulsion and choice in the economic decisions made by individuals or states. The American economic model is surely one of the great sources of its international attractiveness (or in some quarters, opprobrium); this is quite distinct from the question of how the U.S. government uses its economic resources to wield power over others. Even in the case of military force, however, there would seem to be an important soft power dimension that calls for further analysis. Heroic or romantic myths can strongly color the way national (or transnational) military forces are viewed by others, for example, and exercise a strong attraction (consider the continuing flow of would-be martyrs to the banner of Al Qaeda in Iraq today). In the case of the United States, its armed forces have for many years conducted what one might describe as "military diplomacy" in their multi-faceted interactions with foreign militaries as well as in their peacetime "presence" throughout the world.

All of this can lead one to raise a more fundamental question concerning the adequacy of Nye's understanding of soft power in terms (largely if not wholly) of "attraction." Perhaps the term "influence" is better after all at capturing the overall phenomenon we are dealing with here. The French, for example, may be repulsed more than they are attracted by the United States; but this does not necessarily mean that American soft power is ineffective in France. To the extent that the widely discussed process of "globalization" is fundamentally a manifestation of American soft power, it can be argued that American soft power is inexorably shaping the behavior of peoples and governments around the world whether or not they are especially sympathetic to the United States—or indeed, whether or not they are fully aware of the ways in which they are being influenced. Consider in this regard the undeniable success the United States has had since its invasion of Afghanistan and Iraq in promoting democracy and societal reform (particularly reform of education) throughout the Middle East, in spite of what polling data seem to reveal about the virulent hostility of much of the region to the United States and all it stands for. More generally, soft power for Nye seems a fundamentally passive instrument. But public diplomacy, to be truly effective, must be about the active projection of soft power in order to reinforce American influence—or to generate it where otherwise absent.

Nye argues that soft power is a more difficult instrument for governments to wield than hard power, for two reasons: many of its critical resources are outside the control of governments; and soft power tends to "work indirectly by shaping the environment for policy, and sometimes takes years to produce the desired outcomes."[11] This seems broadly true. There can be no question that public diplomacy is limited in what it can do by itself, and also that it is helped immeasurably by a diplomacy that is sensitive to its requirements. As Nye rightly indicates, diplomacy properly understood is an important source of soft power; too often, however, diplomats (and the political leaders they report to) see themselves rather as facilitators and beneficiaries of the hard power instruments of force and money. At the same time, it is probably also true that a public diplomacy that adroitly leverages the cultural resources of its society can under some circumstances afford to do without effective top cover from its nation's diplomacy. In the 1970s, for example, when the American government as a whole pursued a policy of "détente" with the Soviet Union, American public diplomacy receded in some measure in its engagement with the East bloc at a political level; yet it maintained steady pressure against the Soviets at the level of society and culture, and—especially with its new emphasis on the importance of human rights and respect for "civil society" in the East—in some ways increased its effectiveness.

The limited control that a government exercises over its soft power resources has both advantages and disadvantages. Wholly controlled public diplomacy outlets such as state broadcasting operations have the obvious advantage that they are more easily aligned with a government's policy and diplomacy. To the extent that such control is lacking or very loose, on the other hand, there may be significant net gains in terms of the "credibility" of the public diplomacy activities in question and hence their effectiveness with the intended audience.

As regards the actual effects of public diplomacy programs, while it is true that they are notoriously hard to measure and in some cases are very indirect and long term, it is possible to overstate this difficulty. Anecdotal evidence and common sense, if nothing else, suggest that the public diplomacy efforts of the United States and its allies during the Cold War were strikingly successful in creating the conditions that led to the collapse of the Soviet empire in the late 1980s. Moreover, there are some striking cases of relatively direct and short-term results produced by intensive public diplomacy campaigns. The best example is probably the successful American-led effort to counter the Soviet propaganda offensive against NATO's deployment of theater nuclear missiles in Europe in the early 1980s. Instructive also is the case of American radio broadcasting to Poland, which contributed massively to the rise of the Solidarity movement there and to the collapse of Soviet rule over Eastern Europe. The extent to which the Polish service of Radio Free Europe played a virtually operational role in mobilizing the Polish resistance is still not widely understood. There can be little question that it also contributed importantly to the deterrence of Soviet military intervention in Poland, a fateful decision which led in short order to the unraveling of the entire Soviet position in the region.[12]

Clearly, care has to be taken not to oversell the virtues of public diplomacy. In the 20th century, the unprecedented scope and success of Nazi and Soviet propaganda for a time convinced many social scientists and other observers in the West that state-sponsored information programs could be dramatically effective in shaping not only the political environment both domestically and abroad, but ultimately human nature itself. That totalitarian propaganda could persuade its own citizens that "war is peace" and "ignorance is strength"—the mantras of the Ministry of Truth in George Orwell's classic novel *1984*—seemed not at all implausible.[13] But ordinary persons would prove more resistant to propaganda even in closed or totalitarian societies than had been initially supposed, as attested by the popular uprisings against Communist rule in Eastern Europe in the 1950s and 1960s, not to speak of the irreversible growth of dissident movements of varying inspiration there and indeed in the Soviet Union itself in the decades following.

At the same time, there are many reasons for thinking that the impact of public diplomacy during the Cold War was greater than many in the West even today seem prepared to admit. Indeed, an excellent case can be made that the peaceful ending of the Cold War had a great deal to do with the cumulative impact of Western broadcasting and other public diplomacy programs targeting the East Bloc. The loss of faith in Communism as an ideology that was so obvious not only among the mass of the people but even among the very functionaries of the Communist system itself unarguably played a key role in the lack of serious resistance to the revolution from above launched in the Soviet Union in the mid-1980s by President Mikhail Gorbachev.[14]

Perhaps ironically, part of the secret of the West's success in the decades-long "war of ideas" between Communism and democratic capitalism lies precisely in its gradual but finally decisive rejection of the tone, style and approach of classic "propaganda" and its replacement by what has come to be known (since the mid-1970s) as "public diplomacy."[15] Some will say that this is a distinction without a difference, and that the term "public diplomacy" is simply a euphemism to disguise what remains a fundamentally sordid business of manipulation and deception. This is to misunderstand fundamentally the reality of the issue we are dealing with. The nub of the case is nicely stated by Aristotle in his *Rhetoric*, the oldest treatise on this subject and one that is still worth reading: "The things that are truer and better are more susceptible to reasoned argument and more persuasive, generally speaking." The fact of the matter is that the argument for Western-style liberal democracy was and remains a stronger one than the argument for Nazism, Communism, or radical Islamism. This means that public diplomacy need not rely on distortion and manipulation of inconvenient facts to achieve its strategic effect. Much of the power of contemporary public diplomacy in the West can be traced precisely to its known commitment to convey the truth of world events even at some occasional tactical cost to the conveyor. Thus the central importance for American public diplomacy practitioners of maintaining the "credibility" of their programs—and the success they have generally enjoyed in facing down occasional interference in them by policy officials. By contrast, Soviet information efforts were critically hampered until the end not only by a filter of ideological language increasingly remote from the real world, but by a routine resort to classic propaganda techniques often referred to generically as "disinformation." (An extensive program to counter such techniques was one aspect of the public diplomacy offensive undertaken by the United States in the final phase of the Cold War.)[16]

Two arguments are sometimes made nowadays to disparage public diplomacy as a tool of statecraft today. One is that the proliferation of channels of overseas communication in the world today, coupled with the opening up of formerly closed societies in the wake of the fall of the Soviet empire, have essentially made obsolete the information programs of Western governments. The second is that the source of problems for the United States in its relationships abroad is finally not what we "say," but what we "do," and therefore that our attention and resources should be concentrated on fixing poor policies rather than defending them. In the context of the current low standing of the United States in public opinion in the Arab and Muslim world, for example, it is frequently asserted that nothing can truly remedy this problem apart from a basic shift in U.S. policy toward the Arab-Israeli conflict in a direction more favorable to the claims of the Palestinians.

There is no simple answer to this latter argument. At a minimum, it is obviously important to consider the impact of particular policies on public opinion abroad before they are adopted: as USIA Director Edward R. Murrow once famously phrased it, public diplomacy should be in on the takeoffs of policy, not just the crash landings. It is fair to say this has never been done in any systematic way within the U.S. government. On the other hand, public diplomacy surely cannot be allowed to wag the policy dog if the policy is merely unpopular but sound and necessary.[17] And while it is possible that there may be policy choices so misguided that nothing useful can be said in defense or mitigation of them, this is surely the exception rather than the rule. Decisions generally have contexts that are more transparent to American policymakers than to foreigners on their receiving end; these contexts can be identified and explained. In other cases, it will be a question of making appropriate distinctions, signaling intentions, and providing assurances. Public diplomacy, like diplomacy itself, has an important role to play in smoothing the inevitable rough edges of a nation's foreign policy. This having been said, it is also undeniable that public diplomacy is most effective when closely tied to policy—that is, when it is seen as an integral element of a larger policy initiative or campaign, not simply a post hoc rationalization for something an administration has decided to do on other grounds. This is a crucial lesson of some of the signal successes of American public diplomacy in the past (for example, its nuclear and arms control public diplomacy in the early 1980s), one too often overlooked in current discussions of these issues.

As to the first argument, there can be little question that proliferating global communications, and in particular growing access to satellite and cable television and to the internet, are creating a very different and in many ways less welcoming environment for American and other government broadcasting services abroad. In terms of political developments, the collapse of the East Bloc has certainly greatly weakened the rationale underlying Radio Free Europe and Radio Liberty historically—that they function as "surrogate" broadcasting operations in the absence of free domestic media in the target countries. In the case of all U.S. broadcasters, the availability of CNN and other sources of more or less objective news around the world raises a legitimate question as to the extent to which the reportage of news as such should continue to be seen as their priority mission. But two basic points need to be made. First, foreigners look and have always looked to U.S. international broadcasters—particularly but not only the Voice of America—not merely as sources of news but as an authoritative guide to understanding American intentions and actions. This will not change with increasing competition from commercial media. Second, the commercial media for the most part lack any incentive to invest resources in addressing foreigners in their own languages.

Beyond this, however, it is difficult to get around the fact that the commercial competitors of U.S. international broadcasting, while undoubtedly advancing American global interests in certain ways, can in no way be relied upon to present U.S. government actions in a favorable or even strictly neutral light—or indeed to provide objective coverage of the news (consider the widespread complaints about media coverage of the war in Iraq today). In the Arab world, it can be argued that only an American broadcasting presence can be counted on to provide a real alternative to highly distorted and often vitriolically anti-American regional media such as the Qatar-based satellite television station Al-Jazeera. As for the former Soviet Union, a good case can be made for retaining some surrogate broadcasting capability where authoritarian regimes persist (such as Belorus or Turkmenistan) or as a hedge against democratic backsliding and the erosion of free domestic media, a process that seems well underway in contemporary Russia in particular.

The impact of new or emerging technologies on public diplomacy is a large and complex subject; for present purposes, suffice it to say that there does not appear to be a clear net effect of such technologies on the basic utility of public diplomacy as a tool of statecraft.[18] U.S. international broadcasting is no doubt still seen by many as a relic of the short-wave radio era, but in fact it has expanded rapidly into other communications media, including medium-wave radio, satellite television, and the internet (and recent improvements in short-wave technology have sustained its competitiveness even in this medium[19]). Proliferating global communications may in some places cut into its traditional audiences, but also create access to new ones. This is particularly true of the internet with its unique interactivity, which holds great promise for increasing the access of U.S. public diplomacy to key strategic audiences such as the young.

It is important to remember, however, that public diplomacy is but one tool for projecting strategic influence. Other tools, all of which have gained in prominence in the circumstances of the war on terror, include development aid, humanitarian assistance, support for free foreign media, foreign education assistance, and support for democratization, "civil society," and human rights abroad. Very recently, the term "stability and reconstruction operations" has come into vogue in reference to a range of activities undertaken by the U.S. military in collaboration with a variety of other government agencies and non-governmental entities to assist in the rebuilding of state capacities and economic infrastructure in the aftermath of military operations. In all of these cases, as in that of public diplomacy, the U.S. government leverages its soft power by mobilizing private as well as public sector resources to shape economic, social, and political realities in countries throughout the world. In some cases, particularly humanitarian assistance, American motives are primarily altruistic, and little conscious effort is made to exploit the activity for strategic effect. Nevertheless, as became apparent, for example, in the aftermath of the massive military operation organized by the United States to provide relief to the victims of the recent tsunami disaster in Southeast Asia, such programs can often have a more dramatic effect on foreign opinion in a country or region than anything else the United States does there. Typically, bureaucrats in the business of development assistance tend to resist the idea that their efforts can or should have strategic effects or directly serve American policy. Particularly in the context of the requirements of reconstruction in Afghanistan and Iraq, however, it has become clear that such attitudes are simply no longer sustainable. Also increasingly recognized is the central role media and educational reform in the Muslim world have to play in the war against Islamist terrorism.

It is apparent that the American government has barely begun to develop organizational capacities and protocols to address its strategic influence requirements in a comprehensive and coordinated fashion.

In later chapters, some suggestions will be made as to how this situation might be remedied. We now turn to a more detailed discussion of public diplomacy and its relationship to other instruments of what I shall call "psychological-political warfare" and the agencies historically responsible for them.

CHAPTER 3

Public Diplomacy and Psychological-Political Warfare

It was suggested earlier that it is a fundamental mistake to equate "public diplomacy" as practiced by the United States and others today with "propaganda" in the classic sense that term acquired in the practice of Nazi Germany or the Soviet Union. Yet the problem of defining or characterizing public diplomacy hardly ends there. Central to an effective public diplomacy effort is a clear understanding of the scope of public diplomacy and its relationship to kindred disciplines, but the United States has never had anything approaching an operationally adequate doctrine that provides this. The result has been continuing uncertainty and confusion over the roles and missions of public diplomacy and the institutional responsibilities that flow from them.

The most commonly invoked terms bearing on the central meaning of public diplomacy are "information" and "communications." Both of these terms have become seriously overworked in recent years, and in any case do not fully capture this meaning. "Psychological warfare," a term once used virtually synonymously with "propaganda," is now unfashionable if not obsolete; but the term "psychological operations" ("PSYOP") remains in use in the United States (and elsewhere) as the technical expression for communications activities carried out by uniformed military personnel. "Public affairs" is another bureaucratic term of art for the public relations activities of government agencies, with their principal focus on the handling of the domestic media. And finally, there is the term "public diplomacy" itself. What exactly do we mean by it? What precisely is the distinction between public diplomacy and public affairs? In what sense, if any, is it a form of diplomacy as the name implies?

Given the fact that the senior State Department official responsible for public diplomacy has the title "under secretary of State for Public Diplomacy and Public Affairs" and as such also oversees the day-to-day activities of the department's press spokesman, the question must be raised as to just how distinct these functions are and at what point it is proper to intermingle them. In the most general terms, public diplomacy may be said to be more strategic and "proactive," public affairs more tactical and reactive. Public affairs (note that these comments apply as much to the public affairs function at DoD or the White House as to state) is mainly concerned with domestic audiences, and sees as its highest priority maintaining a good press for its organization and leaders. Therefore, the care and feeding of the domestic media tends to preoccupy it; rarely does it seek to shape the news in any sustained way, given the sensitivity of the media to anything perceived as attempted manipulation—though it will certainly cultivate and favor individual reporters and seek to shape their coverage of stories on a day-to-day basis (sometimes through the release or leak of privileged information). Public diplomacy, by contrast, deals exclusively (with a qualification to follow) with international audiences. It too is concerned with breaking news and media coverage, with a focus on the foreign rather than the domestic press. But (at least in theory) it is interested more in the strategic impact of the news on foreign audiences than in providing news for its own sake; it is therefore willing to tailor its news coverage in some measure to the interests, needs, and limitations of its diverse audiences. In addition, of course, it provides various kinds of thematic programming designed, again, for longer-term or strategic effect.

This having been said, a case can also be made that the situation as just described is in fact not ideal, and that public affairs itself needs a strategic component or orientation. The arguments that apply to public diplomacy as a strategic instrument for addressing foreign audiences also apply to public affairs in its relationship to domestic audiences, at least to the extent that the American media cannot be relied on to satisfy fully the government's requirements in this regard. In the 1980s, the Reagan administration created within the State Department an "Office of Latin American Public Diplomacy" of which the primary function was to inform and educate the broad public concerning the threat to American interests in the hemisphere posed by the Sandinista regime in Nicaragua and the Marxist FMLN guerrilla movement in El Salvador. This effort was much criticized at the time as an improper if not actually illegal intervention in the public or (more to the point) the congressional debate then underway on these issues.[1] Yet at a time when wild charges intended to undermine U.S. policy were being generated by organizations of very dubious credibility and then retailed uncritically in the American press, it is not at all clear that the government should have been enjoined from defending itself through such means.[2] Shaping domestic public opinion to confront unrecognized threats to the national security or to accept other desirable if unpopular measures (consider the Carter administration's efforts to "sell" the American people on the Panama Canal treaty in the late 1970s) seems a perfectly legitimate activity, if not indeed a positive obligation of government.

The strategic importance of domestic debates on such issues is currently much in evidence in terms of the war in Iraq. It is clear that the Bush administration has lost much valuable ground by its failure until recently to articulate publicly the case for the war and to develop an effective counterattack on key neuralgic issues such as the failure to uncover Iraqi weapons of mass destruction. As will be discussed in a moment, the question of the propriety of a strategic orientation for Defense Department public affairs remains a key unresolved issue in the current controversy over the nature of "strategic communication."

Diplomacy, whether carried out publicly or in private, involves not simply words but actions—actions that are designed not simply to inform or communicate but to have certain measurable political effects. Public diplomacy frequently addresses a generic global audience, yet it may also be specially targeted. As one observer has put it:

There is a tendency to see public diplomacy as mainly talking...That is about as inadequate a view of public diplomacy as demarching foreign governments is of traditional diplomacy. To be effective, public diplomacy requires action— assertive, aggressive, creative efforts to engage foreign publics, nurture friends, empower allies, build future supporters, and undercut the leverage of America's adversaries.[3]

Public diplomacy specially targeted to well-identified political groups within or across national boundaries—women, youth, religious or business leaders, legislators, political parties, and the like— is sometimes referred to as "political action." I adopt this usage here for the sake of convenience and in the absence of anything better, in spite of its lingering association with certain categories of covert intelligence operations.

Finally, public diplomacy is now generally considered to incorporate the mission often referred to as "educational and cultural affairs," distinguished from its other missions by a longer-term and less policy-relevant focus. Common to both of these areas—and underappreciated by many, who tend to identify public diplomacy with its information component—is face-to-face interaction and the building of relationships, most familiarly in the form of so-called "exchange" programs. Indeed, or so it can be argued, the information component of public diplomacy can only be fully effective where a preexisting relationship nurtures attitudes of trust and belief in the validity of the information being conveyed. Educational and cultural programs are sometimes seen in parochial terms as a benefit primarily to Americans by broadening their international horizons. Yet potentially at least, they also serve an important strategic function by exposing foreign elites to the realities of American life at an impressionable age. Many alumni of American exchange programs have later gone on to high political office in their own countries. Cultural programs are of particular importance as a vehicle for influencing intellectual and opinion-forming elites.[4]

Public diplomacy, then, may be said to have three broad missions: information, political action, and education and culture. Even so understood, however, public diplomacy is only part of a larger arena of statecraft employing the tools of information or communications. There is no accepted term designating this arena. The term "strategic communication" has recently gained some traction within the U.S. government, as already indicated, but to the extent that it is intended to encompass the public affairs function, it remains problematic. As stated above, the term "communication" does not fully capture either the intended psychological impacts of what we are discussing or the political-diplomatic aspects of public diplomacy properly understood. For these reasons, I prefer the invented term "psychological-political warfare," while recognizing that it is far too raw for contemporary bureaucratic use. Euphemism has long been a source of confusion in this field, and at some point must be set aside for the sake of clarity of analysis.

The awkward hyphenation in the term "psychological-political warfare" is intended to capture two distinct though related bureaucratic disciplines with histories extending back to World War II: military psychological operations, and covert political warfare as undertaken by the Central Intelligence Agency (CIA) and its predecessor, the Office of Strategic Services (OSS).[5]

Not since World War II has the military dimension of communication with audiences overseas figured prominently in policy discussions concerning public diplomacy. Few Americans even know that the U.S. Army has maintained, ever since that time, substantial active duty as well as reserve forces dedicated to the "psychological operations" ("PSYOP") mission.[6] Today, however, with the American military virtually continuously engaged in operations around the world in the glare of the global media, with major impact on perceptions of the role and intentions of the United States among allies and adversaries alike, this situation is changing. American military PSYOP campaigns in Afghanistan and Iraq have been very much in the press. Because of the sensitivity of the American commercial media to perceived manipulation of press coverage by the military, this coverage has a tendency to stress the negative (as seen recently in reports that the military had paid for favorable stories to be planted in the Iraqi media).[7]

The traditional PSYOP media remain leaflets, loudspeakers, and radio and television broadcasting. The Fourth Psychological Operations Group (POG), a subordinate element of the U.S. Special Operations Command (USSOCOM) based at Fort Bragg, North Carolina, is an active-duty Army unit that is responsible for developing and producing PSYOP materials and supporting the requirements of joint commanders in the field for communicating with enemy forces or populations. Additional groups with specific regional orientations are housed in the Army reserves, but elements of them are frequently called to active duty. The Air Force also has an important role, both in airdropping PSYOP leaflets and in radio and TV broadcasting from Commando Solo platforms—a squadron of six specially configured EC-130 aircraft operated by the Pennsylvania Air National Guard.

For the most part, psychological operations (in spite of the overtones of this perhaps unfortunate term) are straightforward, simple, highly tactical, and non-controversial—for example, inducements to surrender or warnings to the civilian population to clear an area that is about to be assaulted. Spokesmen for military PSYOP routinely stress the truthful content of PSYOP messages as well as their benign effects in terms of saving lives (the enemy's as much as one's own). To the extent that PSYOP aims at more strategic effects, however, it quickly becomes policy sensitive and tends to attract high-level attention in Washington. At the same time, it becomes difficult to distinguish from public diplomacy, and inevitably raises questions of the appropriate jurisdiction of military and civilian organizations in this area. The recent public flap over planted stories in the Iraqi press involves a relatively new entity within USSOCOM called the Joint Strategic PSYOP Element, which reportedly has a substantial budget to support the work of private contractors who produce (as one did in this case) substantive media products. This is a departure from the past. Typically, PSYOP personnel do not themselves generate or commission written materials or broadcasting scripts of this sort but limit themselves to retransmitting materials produced by U.S. public diplomacy agencies such as the Voice of America.[8]

On the other hand, there is a gray area on the boundary between PSYOP and public diplomacy that has long complicated the institutional handling of these matters. For a period in the mid-1980s and again during the 1991 Gulf War, the Office of the Secretary of Defense (OSD) stood up ad hoc staff elements to undertake a variety of activities that may be described (again, the term has no official standing) as defense public diplomacy. These typically involved validation and declassification of intelligence, preparation of talking points and other materials explaining and defending defense-related policies of the government, the organization of conferences and briefings for foreign audiences of various kinds, and—not least important— systematic counter-propaganda and counter-disinformation campaigns. The last of these was of considerable importance during the Desert Shield phase of the Gulf War in limiting the damage to the coalition cause throughout the Muslim world by Saddam Hussein's hyperactive propaganda machine. The best-known example of the first was the annual publication of a detailed review and analysis of Soviet military developments using sanitized intelligence data, entitled *Soviet Military Power*.[9]

"Strategic communication" is a term that originated recently in the Department of Defense (DoD) as part of a larger effort to improve coordination between military psychological operations, public diplomacy, and public affairs. Problems have bedeviled DoD in this area for many years, but became acute in the context of the terror war and most recently the war in Iraq, where the communications component of coalition postcombat operations has generally and rightly been viewed as disastrous. Again, issues of definition and jurisdiction have been key. Public diplomacy has never had a well-defined, permanent niche within the defense bureaucracy, and existing PSYOP doctrine and practice tend to blur the distinction between these functions. This situation has in turn caused defense public affairs officials to take an uncooperative attitude toward PSYOP and public diplomacy out of concern that association with these disciplines will compromise the integrity of their own operations. Sorting these matters out in a way satisfactory to all concerned remains a major challenge (they will be discussed in more detail in Chapter 9).

Finally, there is the third component of psychological-political warfare, covert political action. In the past, the Central Intelligence Agency has conducted a range of covert operations designed to influence foreign political processes, ranging from the subvention of particular politicians or political parties to support for guerrilla movements to the orchestration of coups d'état. The CIA also has had the capability to carry out what are known as "black propaganda" activities, in the form most significantly of press placements and clandestine radio broadcasting operations. Clandestine broadcasting by states as well as non-state agencies has a long and rich history—one that deserves to be better known.[10] However, by most accounts the CIA today is virtually out of this business. Reportedly, its current propaganda unit has fewer than 25 people—only a tenth of its capability a decade or so ago.[11] Meanwhile, though, the terror war has opened significant new opportunities in this area and created unexpected requirements. The CIA's role in establishing contact and working with the leaders of the Northern Alliance and assorted warlords in Afghanistan contributed importantly to the quick American victory over the Taliban regime. Paramilitary support for irregular forces along these lines has been a fixture of CIA political warfare since the early days of OSS involvement in the French resistance against the Nazis in World War II.

A fertile source of confusion in this area is the common assumption that clandestinity in psychological-political warfare necessarily implies distorting or concealing truth in ways that are not done by overt information programs. In fact, the classic distinction between "white" and "black" propaganda has nothing to do with the substantive truth of the material being communicated, but only with whether the source of the material is openly and accurately acknowledged: "black" propaganda is defined by the fact that it purports to be from a source that is not the real one (in a classic example, from a bogus organization of military deserters). ("Gray" propaganda, on the other hand, is information neither openly acknowledged nor misleadingly attributed. Much British propaganda in the United States during World War I, for example, was of this character.)

At the same time, it is important not to be misled by American or other defenders of psychological-political warfare into supposing that its various disciplines do or should communicate only "truth." In the commercial world, "truth in advertising" hardly requires companies to emphasize ways in which their products are inferior to the competition's. Effective propaganda certainly needs to avoid lies in the sense of counterfactual statements, but it must also be selective in what it chooses to communicate. Indeed, in this respect there is not a sharp difference between PSYOP, public diplomacy, or even public affairs—or for that matter, the routine practices of the commercial media (consider, again, the extreme selectivity of much current media coverage of the war in Iraq). The moral calculus affecting these matters is therefore by no means so clear as it is generally made out to be by the critics of government information programs.

A further point needs to be made about the strategic context of psychological-political warfare. In modern times, the systematic employment by democratic governments of propaganda, military psychological operations, and covert political warfare was originally limited almost entirely to wartime. Following World War II, the United States came very close to divesting itself completely of the capabilities in these areas it had created during the war. It thought better of doing so as a result of the growing Soviet military and political threat in Europe and the outbreak of war in Korea in 1950. Over the course of the Cold War, however, there was considerable fluctuation in the strategic environment and corresponding uncertainty as to the exact role of these capabilities and whether they were in fact fully legitimate instruments of statecraft. To speak of psychological-political "warfare" in this context is therefore somewhat problematic, and a more neutral term (such as "activities") would perhaps be preferable. In any case, use of this term is not meant to imply that these capabilities were always cultivated or used only against adversaries of the United States. Indeed, their effective use to influence neutrals or even allies has always been an important challenge—and often one with greater tangible payoff. As we shall see shortly, this is still very much the case today.

Let us return to the question of the relation between public diplomacy and diplomacy proper. To repeat what was said earlier, public diplomacy is most effective when it is closely integrated with policy, rather than being simply an afterthought or post hoc justification of policy. In spite of the obvious tension between diplomacy and public diplomacy, public diplomacy can also—and should—be supported by diplomacy. Ambassadors, for example, can lend their personal presence and voice in their particular countries to public diplomacy campaigns;[12] diplomatic demarches can be crafted to reinforce in private with foreign governments the arguments made in public statements emanating from officials in Washington. (Moreover, though this point is not made often enough, public diplomacy can support diplomacy. A difficult negotiation can sometimes be made easier by ratcheting up public pressure on a foreign government through public diplomacy channels or the domestic media.) At times in the past, American administrations have launched diplomatic initiatives whose fundamental purpose was to affect international opinion rather than to reach agreement. Dwight Eisenhower, who was keenly attuned to this dimension of diplomacy through his involvement in psychological warfare during World War II, launched the Atoms for Peace and Open Skies initiatives in the 1950s primarily for reasons of psychological-political strategy, as a way of gaining the moral high ground relative to the Soviet Union and enhancing the standing of the United States in the contest with the Soviets in the third world.[13]

This leads to a further point concerning the direct role of the White House and the president himself in public diplomacy. Presidents are a very important public diplomacy asset. Even when presidents address domestic audiences, as they do most of the time, they are overheard by foreigners, so that they and their speechwriters need to keep in mind the sensitivities of foreign audiences. Occasions for addressing foreign audiences directly (for example, interviews with the foreign press or speeches given on overseas trips) should be sought out and used for strategic public diplomacy purposes. Further, what presidents do often matters as much as what they say. Presidents engage in a varied array of symbolic behaviors (laying of wreaths, reviewing troops, and the like) that need to be seen as an integral part of American public diplomacy. Ronald Reagan's extraordinary speech in France on the 40th anniversary of the Normandy invasion exemplifies these too often forgotten or missed opportunities.[14]

CHAPTER 4

Strategic Influence in the Age of Terror

Let us move from these general considerations to look more closely at the role of strategic influence in the contemporary security environment. Is public diplomacy or strategic influence broadly understood in fact as an effective instrument in the war on terror? What strategy should the United States be pursuing in this area? Are we making sensible assumptions about the character of our target audiences and how they are likely to react to our efforts to influence them? What specific approaches or types of operations are apt to have the highest payoff or be most cost-effective? Which run the risk of proving counterproductive? Broadening out from the terror war proper, the discussion will consider in addition the larger question of the global image of the United States and whether or in what ways it can or should be nurtured by strategic influence efforts. I will focus particularly on the neglected question of strategies for influencing our traditional European allies and, more broadly, what might be called the emerging global elite.

Strategic influence at first sight seems hardly the weapon of choice in dealing with the threat of catastrophic terrorism, as fanatical terrorist adversaries do not seem good candidates for reasoned persuasion or dialogue. If we can influence the behavior of terrorists at all, or so it is generally assumed, it is only through the threat or use of military force;

and even that may be insufficient to deter a fanatical suicide bomber. Yet the matter is not quite so simple. While some proportion of our terrorist opponents may indeed be undeterrable, there is also likely to be significant variation in their susceptibility to external messages. One such message, delivered by some combination of force and persuasive speech, might be the simple one: "your cause is futile"—a message whose power is bound to increase the longer the fight continues with few measurable gains for the terrorists. Another—less palatable no doubt but of proven effectiveness within traditional Arab cultures (it has been used in various forms by the Israelis, for example, in their bulldozing of houses of suicide bombers)—might be "your family will suffer for your actions." In the past, surprising success has sometimes been achieved by programs that use defectors from terrorist or guerrilla organizations to demoralize their former compatriots—consider especially the *pentiti* ("repenters") of the Italian Red Brigades in the 1970s.[1] In Iraq, the government recently organized a television show featuring the confessions of former terrorists; the show has proven wildly popular.[2] More generally, there are a variety of techniques of classical psychological warfare that can be used to attack an opposing organization by sowing confusion, suspicion, and enmity in its ranks and turning its leaders against one another. Judging at least from the public record, there is little reason to believe that the United States has made significant use of any of these measures in its current struggle with Islamist radicalism.[3]

The primary application of strategic influence in the terror war nevertheless lies not here but rather in its effect on the strategic environment that creates and nurtures terrorists. The winning of the "hearts and minds" of those who are less than fully committed to terrorist action must therefore be the centerpiece of any long-term effort to attack the sources of terrorism in contemporary Arab and Islamic societies, as indeed has been broadly recognized within the U.S. government as well as among outside observers. Such an effort should encompass an appeal both to mass audiences in the Muslim world and to the political and cultural elites there who have too often tolerated or actively abetted the rise of radical Islamism throughout the world. Yet, realistically, what are the prospects of the United States making any significant impact on public opinion in that part of the world?

There can be little question that the current standing of the United States in the eyes of Muslims generally, and Arabs in particular, is at an all-time low. Opinion polling designed to elicit popular attitudes on elemental questions such as whether the United States is viewed "favorably" or "unfavorably" generally show support ranging from negligible to modest, even in countries traditionally friendly to this country such as Turkey, Egypt, or Jordan. The invasion of Iraq in the spring of 2003 clearly marked a significant negative turning point in this regard. However, popular reactions in many parts of the Middle East even to the events of 9/11 and the U.S. intervention in Afghanistan shortly thereafter had already revealed widespread lack of sympathy for the United States and lack of support for its actions against Al-Qaeda and the Taliban regime. For example, a Gallup poll taken in the Islamic world during December 2001 and January 2002 indicated, among other things, that only 18% of those polled believed that the 9/11 attacks were carried out by Arabs, and that only 9% thought American military action in Afghanistan morally justified.[4] It is widely claimed that America's unpopularity in the region is largely explained by its long-standing support for Israel in its dispute with its various Arab neighbors over the years. There is also a general perception that the United States is out to dominate the Middle East because of its oil, and for this reason props up a variety of corrupt and subservient Arab regimes there. Further reinforcing this idea is of course the greatly expanded American military presence and activity in the Persian Gulf since the 1991 war with Iraq.

The undeniable reality of much of this picture would be bad enough. However, it is greatly magnified by two other factors, one traditional, the other recent. The first is the Arab penchant for conspiratorial thinking, which attributes to the United States a virtually all-seeing, all-knowing presence in the region and hidden and corrupt motives of the most fantastic kinds.[5] The second is the dramatic expansion of Arabic-language satellite television broadcasting in the last decade. It is hard to overstate the impact throughout the Middle East of Al-Jazeera in particular, a television station established in Qatar under the aegis of the royal family (and with some financial support from it), but operating—uniquely for the region—with journalistic autonomy and a sensationalistic approach in both the format and content of its programs.[6] Al-Jazeera's relentlessly one-sided coverage of the Palestinian *intifada* has clearly inflamed anti-Israeli (and by association, anti-American) sentiment around the region, and helped make it wildly popular (regular viewership is now upwards of 35 million people). Its coverage of the war on terror and the U.S. military occupation of Iraq have given Al-Qaeda a vital platform for its propaganda, while filling the airwaves with graphic scenes of devastation and carnage inflicted by American forces together with much biased and inflammatory commentary on the situation in Iraq. American officials have repeatedly made clear their displeasure with Al-Jazeera. In spite of the close relationship the United States maintains with the government of Qatar (where it has a major air base), however, it seems to have been unwilling or unable to do anything about this state of affairs.[7]

This overall picture has led some knowledgeable observers to a position of deep pessimism regarding the ability of the United States to affect contemporary Arab opinion in any significant way. As the distinguished American academic Fouad Ajami has put it: "It's hopeless. We will not get a hearing. I think we are deeply alienated from these societies, in the extreme.... Our sins are very evident... our good deeds are never really taken in, never factored in." In an extended analysis of Al-Jazeera, Ajami underlines its fundamental hostility to the United States in spite of its veneer of Western journalism.[8] Others have argued that it is a waste of time for American officials to appear there. In an effort to counter the appeal of Al-Jazeera, the United States has invested substantial funds in its own Arabic-language satellite TV service, Al-Hurra. So far, however, this does not seem to have made significant inroads given the formidable nature of the competition and the evident limitations of its own credibility. But quite apart from the Al-Jazeera issue, many observers seem convinced that short of major changes in American policy in the region—above all, resolution of the Palestinian issue and the withdrawal of American military forces from the Persian Gulf—Muslim public opinion will remain implacably hostile.

In fact, it is much too soon to despair of Muslim opinion, and therefore of American strategic influence efforts in the Middle East or the wider Muslim world. For one thing, the United States has been very late getting into this game. For another, the American presence in the Middle East over the past fifteen years has overwhelmingly been a military one, with the imperial overtones that inevitably suggests. But there is every reason to think this presence will be transitory, certainly in its current massive and intrusive form. Indeed, one of the less obvious benefits of the second Gulf War and the overthrow of the regime of Saddam Hussein has been to allow the United States to liquidate virtually its entire military presence in Saudi Arabia—a key neuralgic issue used to much effect against the United States by Islamist radicalism; and the U.S. has made clear it does not aspire to maintain permanent bases in Iraq.[9] Moreover, the United States has had at best limited opportunities for advertising the benign character of

American power in the region. As (or assuming that) the security situation in Iraq stabilizes and American forces are drawn down, the imperial edge on the current American image will be softened. At the same time, the fruits of the enormous material investments in that country so far made by the U.S. government (and private sector) will become increasingly visible, both in Iraq itself and throughout the region. Recently, there have been several striking demonstrations of the malleability of public opinion in the Muslim world in the face of the reality of American beneficence. Hardly any country in the Muslim world has been as thoroughly penetrated by Islamist attitudes and as hostile to the United States as Pakistan. And yet, humanitarian assistance delivered by the American military to Pakistani victims of the devastating October 2005 earthquake had an immediate and dramatic positive impact on the overall American image there—doubling the percentage of those polled saying they viewed the United States favorably. Similarly, the highly visible American aid to Indonesia following the tsunami of December 2004 caused a sharp spike in the favorability rating of the United States in that country.[10]

A further reason for optimism concerning America's prospects for engaging and influencing Muslim public opinion has to do with the missteps of the terrorists themselves. There is good reason for thinking that the appeal of Al-Qaeda throughout much of the Islamic world may have peaked and started on a downward trajectory. Annual polling in the Middle East by the Pew Global Attitudes Project, the source for most of the gloomy statistics on Muslim opinion since 2001, this year showed not only an increase in favorability ratings for the United States in countries like Lebanon, Pakistan, and Jordan, but a decline in support for Osama bin Laden virtually everywhere. The poll found that "nearly three-quarters of Moroccans and roughly half of those in Pakistan, Turkey, and Indonesia see Islamic extremism as a threat to their countries."[11] Support for suicide bombing and for violence against innocent civilians has also shown significant decline. This clearly reflects a growing revulsion against the gruesome terrorist tactics used in Iraq by the jihadist leader Abu Musab al-Zarqawi and widely publicized on Arab television. The al-Zarqawi-inspired suicide bomb attacks on two hotels in Amman, Jordan, in November 2005, which killed numerous guests at a local wedding, led to street demonstrations by thousands of Jordanians and denunciation of the Jordanian-born al-Zarqawi by members of his own extended family. There are also encouraging signs of movement by Islamic clerics in various countries, including Saudi Arabia, to condemn jihadist violence more clearly and vocally. In this respect, it seems fair to say that the war for the soul of Islam sought by the terrorists, far from being over, has in fact barely begun.[12]

But it is also essential to realize that the long isolation of the people of the Arab world from the global information grid is only now coming to an end, and with effects little short of spectacular. In spite of all the problems it has caused the United States, Al-Jazeera and its increasingly numerous imitators have brought about what is almost certainly an irreversible revolution in the regional media environment.[13] In the long run, this revolution seems very likely to prove a net benefit to the United States. Already, though, Al-Jazeera's constant challenge to established authority throughout the Arab world, its extensive coverage, for example, of the Iraqi elections, its willingness to give air time to Israeli officials, and even more significantly, the serious attention it is now giving to covering and explaining the American political process, have arguably transformed it from a liability to an asset for the United States. Other rival stations, notably the Dubai-based Al-Arabiya, are also moving in the direction of greater professionalism and a more balanced approach to covering things American.[14] These outlets are in effect promoting American soft power in the Arab world in ways that the United States itself is currently incapable of doing.

How can the United States leverage American soft power generally in order to advance the current security agenda of the United States in the Muslim world? Instead of rehearsing the various menus of programmatic activities proposed in recent studies of this subject, this discussion will limit itself to identifying briefly the major strategic areas that I believe hold the key to success in the terror war, but that are being exploited inadequately if at all by the United States at the present time. These are as follows: ideological engagement on terrorism and the terror war, ideological engagement on Israel, the Jews, and the Israeli-Palestinian dispute, ideological engagement on liberalism, democracy, and market economics, regional media policy and strategy, education reform, and support for political reform, state-building, civil society, and democratization.

IDEOLOGICAL ENGAGEMENT ON TERRORISM AND THE TERROR WAR

For reasons that are entirely understandable, the Bush administration opted in the aftermath of 9/11 to consider itself in a "war" with "terrorism." This decision has since been criticized from several directions. Some have argued that characterizing the war on terror as "war" actually hurts the cause by elevating terrorists to the status of "warriors" who, as such, are a worthy opponent deserving of a certain respect (and may also have complicated their legal status when captured), and perhaps by giving an appearance of overreaction. Others have questioned the use of the word "terrorism," which as commonly noted describes a tactic rather than a concrete enemy. Yet the administration felt it would be unwise to declare "war" against an enemy it would have to identify in some sense as Islam. Very recently, however, this decision has been revisited, and the president has made a series of speeches to the American public that set out with much greater candor the administration's view of why we are at war and the nature of the enemy. For the first time, he has laid out the parallel between Islamic radicalism or jihadism and the global challenge of communism.[15] This move has also attracted some criticism for unduly exaggerating the potential appeal of bin Laden-style Islamism,[16] but on balance it is surely a step in the right direction. It is surely time to name the enemy, and not merely with the name "Osama bin Laden," who is now almost certainly irrelevant to the progress and outcome of the war on terror (although killing or capturing him nevertheless continues to hold high symbolic value). Beyond that, however, the United States has to do much better in articulating its overall view of the nature of radical Islamism, its relationship to Islam as such, and its relationship to terrorism as a tactic and to the use of violence generally to achieve its aims. American government spokesmen obviously have to be careful not to give the impression of lecturing Muslims on how to practice their religion. But there is much they could say with perfect propriety about the dubious religious basis and authority of jihadism and its contamination by currents of non-Islamic thought such as fascism or European-style left nihilism. And there is a great deal to be said about why terrorism is abhorrent. This includes taking on the notion, still widely accepted among Arabs, that terrorism is an unfortunate but necessary weapon in the struggle against Israel. Perhaps the key point is the importance of taking our Muslim interlocutors seriously on their own terms and showing them the consideration of arguing with them.

A second and related issue concerns the rationale for the invasion of Iraq by the United States and the overthrow of the regime of Saddam Hussein. There is no need to belabor the difficulties the Bush administration has had to wrestle with here, or its evident embarrassment over the failure of American forces to turn up the weapons of mass destruction touted by prewar intelligence or to establish a clear linkage between the Saddam regime and international jihadist terrorism. But there are certainly things that can be said in mitigation of these failures and on behalf of the administration's turn to a doctrine of preemptive or preventive war following 9/11. In the absence of any plausibly argued case, Iraqis and other Arabs are invited to continue spinning conspiracy theories of one sort or another. Moreover, the United States needs to pay close attention to the developing image of the former regime both in Iraq and in the region. The trial of Saddam does not seem to be attracting much attention in this country, but its conduct and outcome will be of great importance in laying to rest the Ba'athist movement and establishing the legitimacy of the new regime and America's support for it. Documentation of the crimes of Saddam and the inner character of the former regime needs to be given greater priority as well. What is more, the enormous quantities of documents of the Saddam era captured by American forces since 2003 may yet vindicate American claims about weapons of mass destruction and Iraqi ties to terrorism, if properly exploited by the United States for public diplomacy purposes—something that has so far failed to occur, for reasons that are unclear.[17]

IDEOLOGICAL ENGAGEMENT ON ISRAEL, THE JEWS, AND THE ISRAELI-PALESTINIAN DISPUTE

Critics of American public diplomacy today are generally quick to emphasize the negative impact of American support for Israel on its image in the Middle East; but they assume there is nothing to be done about this other than increasing American diplomatic pressure on the Israelis to accept or accommodate Palestinian demands. Little attention is ever paid to the possibility of an enhanced American public diplomacy effort on this front. The truth of the matter is that both the United States and Israel itself have almost totally neglected the public diplomacy instrument in this context.[18] Yet it is far from the case that Israel's treatment of the Palestinians, or more generally the foreign and security policies it has pursued in the region, are indefensible. At Camp David and later in Oslo, Israeli negotiators made historic concessions in the direction of accepting a Palestinian state meeting all but maximalist Palestinian requirements. Nor does the United States have to make apologies for the role it has played in the region in the past. It has by no means always simply supported the Israeli government, but has tried to be an honest broker between the parties if and where circumstances permitted;[19] and let us remember that the current American administration as well as the consensus view in Israel itself now favors an eventual Palestinian state. This leads to a more general point. Arabs, even Arab elites, have little real knowledge of the contemporary history of the Middle East. Serious historical scholarship on the region is virtually monopolized by Americans, Europeans, and Israelis in works that are rarely translated into Arabic. Devising ways to provide Arab audiences with balanced, myth-free accounts of their own history, and of the real role of the United States in it, is one of the great yet largely unrecognized challenges facing us in this arena.[20] One intriguing approach might be to bring together scholars from different countries within the region to produce a single consensus-based history of their relations—as has recently been done in Northeast Asia.[21]

Beyond the question of national policies, however, are more fundamental existential issues concerning the legitimacy of the state of Israel, anti-Semitism and Holocaust-denial, and the historic relationship of Jews and Arabs. These issues have recently been put in play in the region in a dramatic manner by the new ultra-hard line of the president of Iran, Mahmoud Ahmadinejad.[22] There is some encouragement in the negative reactions voiced by some Arabs (and for that matter Iranians) to Ahmadinejad's inflammatory remarks about relocating the Jews to a new home in Europe and denying the Holocaust. It has to be kept in mind that Jews and Judaism have an honored place in the Koran, one not easily effaced by literalist-minded jihadis. It is surely time for Christians, Jews, and reasonable Muslims to begin to map out strategies for increasing understanding and cooperation between the "peoples of the book." One possible focus for such efforts could be the status of religious sites in Israel/Palestine in the context of a final settlement of the conflict there. What role governments can or should have in any of this is of course a question, but it can be argued that some involvement by them could well be essential.[23]

IDEOLOGICAL ENGAGEMENT ON LIBERALISM, DEMOCRACY, AND MARKET ECONOMICS

Too often, public diplomacy is identified with factual information that paints a picture of the United States or presents the elements of its policies abroad. Following 9/11, Charlotte Beers, the new under secretary of state in charge of public diplomacy, recognized that such an approach was insufficient, and pushed a series of programs designed to "brand" America as a land of tolerance and diversity. But it is surely less important to persuade foreigners that Americans are a kind and gentle people than that the United States knows what it is doing when it sets about to spread democracy and the American way of life around the world, and is capable of presenting arguments in support of those things. The ongoing American project of implanting democracy in two nations that have never known it is likely to have a large if not decisive impact on the future course of the terror war. Much of the public spotlight here has focused of course on elections, since they are the most visible manifestation of democratic development. However, stable democracy in Afghanistan and Iraq will require a great deal more, beginning with a constitution establishing the framework of a liberal democracy in the specifically modern sense. The constitution- and institution-building processes that continue in both countries are rich sources of instruction not only for their own people but for Muslims everywhere. And yet little seems to have been done by the United States to highlight or publicize these processes, or for that matter, to bring to bear lessons from its own history that might have relevance to them. In general, efforts by the U.S. government to convey information and argument on the conceptual and historical basis of contemporary liberal democracy and its characteristic institutions to Muslim audiences have been crude or non-existent. Once again, there is a question of how much the government can in propriety do in such matters, as distinct from private sector experts or politicians, for example; but at the very least it can facilitate their efforts. Any sophisticated strategy in this area would need to begin from the recognition that it is a mistake to hold up the American model as the best or only one, or to present the American experience in wholly triumphal terms. Muslims have good reasons for being suspicious of Western liberalism and the secularism and license to which many feel it inevitably leads. There are difficult and delicate issues here for Americans to deal with, such as the impact of Hollywood movies and morals on other cultures. At the same time, the United States should not shy away from highlighting aspects of its own experience that may have special relevance for political modernization in the Middle East. In particular, the strong presidency of the American constitutional system may well be better suited to fractious societies such as Iraq or Afghanistan than the European parliamentary model.[24]

Some additional remarks are in order on the question of free market economic policies and the extent to which they should be embraced and made central in any American public diplomacy or influence strategy. Free market economics are not well understood or appreciated in relatively traditional societies like Iraq or Afghanistan, where tribal or family bonds tend rather to support some vaguely defined "socialist" ideology at the national level. Moreover, the growing anti-globalization movement constitutes a direct challenge to widely shared free market ideas, particularly free trade. Partly because of the awkward questions sometimes raised by some illiberal practices of professing free market nations (agricultural subsidies being a prominent example), and partly because of the domestic political disputes that so frequently occur over these matters, the United States and other Western governments do not seem to have had much stomach for giving economic issues a prominent place in their public diplomacy or democracy-building efforts. A good case can be made that this situation is no longer sustainable. Particularly where nations accepting foreign economic assistance are held to increasingly higher standards of transparency, rectitude, and fidelity to policies defined by donors or international financial institutions, it becomes more important to foster public understanding of measures that otherwise could generate internal political opposition and weaken emerging democratic institutions. One important resource in this regard that has not been sufficiently mobilized by the U.S. government in the past is American businessmen operating abroad or in multinational corporations.

Central to any effective strategy in this area is simply making available in Arabic translation (and in other strategic languages of the Muslim world) key works of Western history, political philosophy, and the social sciences that explain and support the Western liberal model. Some private efforts are underway along these lines, but much more needs to be done, and almost certainly with some official sponsorship and coordination.[25]

REGIONAL MEDIA POLICY AND STRATEGY

A fundamental issue, though one that has not been very much discussed at least in public, is what overall posture or policy the United States should adopt regarding Al-Jazeera and other regional and local media in the Middle East and throughout the Muslim world. I have suggested that Al-Jazeera's impact may be more benign at least in the long run than is usually thought, but the fact remains that its behavior continues to raise serious questions.[26] Though the United States has chosen to compete against this and other Arab-operated media (via the Arabic-language Radio Sawa and Al Hurra television as well as the

Iraqi Media Network operating out of Baghdad), a more promising strategy may be to embrace them—attempting to develop more cooperative relationships while continuing to monitor their content closely and exerting appropriate pressures. One prong of such a strategy in the longer term is to put significant resources into the training of Arab journalists in professional standards and practices and in knowledge of the real world. There may well be possibilities for program placement or even collaborative programming with these broadcasting organizations, especially given the shaky financial condition of many of them, including Al-Jazeera itself.[27]

The problem of foreign media policy for the United States is especially acute when and where shooting starts. It is relatively clear from recent conflicts (going back to American air operations against Serbia in the 1990s) that there is no doctrine or real consensus within the U.S. government regarding the use of military force against civilian communications targets such as national radio and television stations. Yet arguably there are times when the appropriate response to an adversary's propaganda is not counterpropaganda but rather precision bombing at its source (or at the soft end of the "kinetic" spectrum, electronic jamming). Government-sponsored "hate radios" in Rwanda a decade ago were centrally responsible for an orgy of massacres that cost hundreds of thousands of lives; these radios could have been put out of business by a few sorties of modern aircraft. In Iraq in 2003, the U.S. military permitted "Baghdad Bob" to broadcast from the Iraqi Ministry of Information until well into the invasion, though admittedly these broadcasts were so ludicrous that they probably caused little real harm. Throughout the Iraqi conflict, Al-Jazeera had reporters on the ground broadcasting material that routinely placed the United States in the worst possible light, and in some cases seemed deliberately calculated to inflame sentiment against this country both in Iraq itself and throughout the Arab world. Yet the United States did essentially nothing to counter activities that in any objective sense were hostile, and that in some cases directly impacted the course of military operations and threatened American lives. Nor did the United States do very much to try to control even the worst excesses of the free Iraqi media that began to proliferate at the end of combat operations. The question has to be asked whether all this occurred as a matter of strategic judgment or merely in reaction to perceived political problems that might arise at home should the military go down that road. A case can surely be made that the U.S. erred in a major way in not restricting the activities particularly of Al-Jazeera reporters[28] and at the extreme, expelling them from the country. There is also a question of whether the United States should have jammed objectionable telecasts, assuming the technical means for doing so were available.[29] These are non-destructive steps that would have been highly defensible politically, certainly within the region. In any case, these are issues that urgently need to be revisited in any effort to create a coherent and effective national policy in this important but highly sensitive area.

Of course, the United States is bound to be better off if it does not have to act directly against foreign media outlets. The alternative is to pressure the governments that control or host these outlets to rein them in or, at the extreme, suppress them. Predictably and with some justification, the United States has been reluctant to take diplomatic actions that appear to contradict its often loudly proclaimed adherence to the idea of free speech and a free press. On the other hand, we are here speaking of media that are, to begin with, virtually if not wholly controlled by their own governments, such as those of Egypt or Saudi Arabia. This means that these governments are seriously complicit when these outlets broadcast, as they have routinely done, distorted and hate-filled material about American policies and actions in the Middle East. Making a diplomatic issue out of such behavior therefore seems entirely appropriate.

EDUCATION REFORM

It has been widely recognized that perhaps the most serious long-term challenge facing the United States in the war on terror is to reverse the trend in the Islamic world toward the domination of its institutions of higher education by radical Islamism in its various forms. In particular, the role of religious schools—so-called "*madrasas*"—as breeding grounds of jihadism is well known.[30] There are obviously many sensitivities to be faced here, particularly if the United States is seen as in any way shaping or suppressing the way Islam is taught to Muslims. Yet the baleful influence of religious dogmatism and its direct contribution to terrorist recruitment is not the only shortcoming of contemporary Arab education. The lack of attention to science and technology, to economics and the other social sciences at all levels of education is a major contributor to the underdevelopment of Arab societies. The lack of knowledge of recent history and politics feeds the various pathologies of contemporary Arab opinion—for example, as just noted, relating to the Arab-Israeli conflict. These problems are not unrecognized in the Arab world itself, and American assistance in addressing them is apt to be more welcome.[31]

Student exchange programs are an integral component of any larger effort to influence education in the Middle East and the wider Muslim world. There are, to be sure, difficult practical issues associated with such programs; in the context of the terror war, screening young Arab men for visas to enter the United States is a vexing problem. Less obvious but equally deserving of attention is the question of exactly what educational environment is being provided for Muslim students in the United States and how any adverse impacts of American culture on such students can be minimized. It is well to remember that the Egyptian Sayyid Qutb, one of the founders of contemporary jihadism, spent several years in the United States in the 1940s and developed in the process a profound hatred for American liberalism and all its works.[32] That mere exposure to life and to educational opportunities in advanced democratic societies will have desirable effects on young Muslims is in any case belied massively by the experience of Muslim immigrants in Western Europe: upwardly mobile Muslims enrolled in engineering schools and other technical studies there have proven particularly susceptible to jihadist recruitment. All of this suggests the need to rethink traditional approaches in this area radically.

SUPPORT FOR POLITICAL REFORM, STATE-BUILDING, CIVIL SOCIETY, AND DEMOCRATIZATION

It has not been customary, as noted earlier, to consider democratization and related policies as aspects of public diplomacy or influence operations, but rather as something more akin to development aid or humanitarian assistance—as generic activities intended primarily to benefit the recipient, and the donor only secondarily if at all. Put another way, they have tended not to be viewed within a strategic framework. Indeed, many foreign policy traditionalists have held that if anything, they work against American strategic interests, at least in the near term. This is particularly true of democratization in the context of the Middle East, which of all regions of the world has been the most resistant to it. There, the opening up of the autocratic political systems that have long dominated the region threatens to empower religious populists rather than liberal reformers, and therefore to create political space for radical Islamism that does not now exist (as in the success of Hamas candidates in the January 2006

Palestinian elections). Moreover, there is always the danger that active promotion of democracy by the United States will be seen in the Middle East as part of a larger imperial project and prove counter-productive in terms of influencing opinion and changing attitudes.

While it cannot be denied that there are still serious questions as to whether or to what extent the growth of democracy in the Middle East is really in American interests, it seems increasingly clear that such concerns have been overstated. American-sponsored democratization in the region seems to be pushing on an open or at worst half-closed door, in the sense that there is little evident resistance to it in any ideologically coherent form. The occasional anti-democratic rants by Al-Qaeda figures such as al-Zarqawi do not seem to resonate among the broad Arab masses, and Ba'athism at any rate is hardly a credible alternative. Moreover, the United States has been rather better at organizing "coalitions of the willing" to promote democracy in the Middle East than to wage war there. This is particularly true of the Europeans, who have been generally supportive of American reform initiatives in the region and thereby have largely undercut charges of American unilateralism or imperialism. Of course, a great deal remains to be done on this front. But the overall political climate in the region seems much more favorable to democratic reform than ever before. The case of Iraq certainly shows that democracy has proven attractive enough to broad segments of the population in a country that has never known it; and the signs are encouraging that the Iraqis will work out a democratic destiny among themselves, though of course the jury is still out on this. Functioning democracies in Iraq as well as Afghanistan are certain in turn to have an enormous long-term effect on political attitudes and behavior throughout the entire region. Even in the near term, however, there are many signs of movement in the Arab world in the direction of broadened political participation, even in the most conservative regimes (notably, Saudi Arabia).[33]

Yet the skeptics do have reason to worry about the hijacking of emerging democracies in the Middle East by the Islamists. This is why it is important that democratization be seen in a larger context and pursued with due consideration for the strategic picture. Political progress in the Arab world should not be defined by elections alone, but rather in terms of the growth of liberal political institutions, the rule of law, state bureaucracies that are efficient and uncorrupt, and perhaps most important, a vibrant "civil society" that can act as a check on arbitrary state power or totalitarian religious impulses.

Understood in these terms, however, it becomes clear that democratization is an intricate construct, one that needs to be articulated and explained at various levels of abstraction for audiences of different capacities as well as tailored to the circumstances of particular countries. In other words, democratization, if it is to be effective, must in the first place be communicated effectively—that is to say, must be fully integrated into the larger public diplomacy efforts of the U.S. government and its partners in this arena (especially, again, the Europeans).

Let us turn now, more briefly, to consider the role of public diplomacy and influence operations more generally in American policy outside the Middle East. Of critical importance here, though very largely neglected today, are the attitudes of publics in erstwhile friendly advanced democracies that have become increasingly estranged from the United States and hostile to its international role, especially those of Western Europe. As one observer has tellingly noted, "the most stunning reaction to our Iraq enterprise did not come, as so many had predicted, from the Arab Street, but from the European Street."[34] This applies particularly to the opinion-forming components in these societies—and more broadly, to what may be called the emerging transnational European and European-influenced elite, which is well on its way to creating a distinctive political and intellectual outlook that is in many ways profoundly at odds with core American values. The ignorance of all things American in the Arab world is difficult to exaggerate; but we need to be equally sensitive to the lack of real understanding of or sympathy toward the United States in today's Europe. French and German anti-Americanism regularly takes forms as hysterical as anything to be found in the Middle East,[35] but even many educated Britons share grossly caricatured ideas of the United States. Political and cultural communications across the Atlantic are at their lowest ebb since World War II.[36]

Americans have become increasingly accustomed to taking a dismissive approach to European views and concerns. Unfortunately, even on a cold-eyed analysis, Europe cannot be dismissed or taken for granted. Unpalatable as it may be to face the fact, Europe collectively has great potential for harming American interests around the world in the longer term—indeed, perhaps more than any other great power (if the European Union can be so described). This applies not only to the Europeans' willingness to act as genuine partners in the war against terror (in which their own societies are and will remain a major battlefield and staging area due to their burgeoning Muslim populations), as vital as that is for us. It reflects the distinct albeit distant possibility that Europe will continue on its current trajectory toward greater political unity and cultural homogeneity and will increasingly come to regard itself as an alternative "West," and at the extreme, as the central pillar and organizer of a global alliance against the United States. Such an alliance might extend not only to other major powers such as Russia, but to non-state actors such as global media, global business elites, non-governmental organizations, and the machinery of the United Nations. It should be a fundamental objective of American diplomacy and public diplomacy alike in the coming years to ensure that such a scenario does not materialize.

To explore tactical and technical options for engaging European opinion would take us too far afield, but several points may be made. First and most importantly, what is needed is clearly not a Cold War-style mass communications effort but rather one specifically targeting opinion-forming elites, and therefore more intellectually and culturally sophisticated than has generally been true of American public diplomacy.[37] Imaginative use of new communications technologies should be an important aspect of any such effort, as well as techniques (particularly interactivity) that they enable. Journalists, businessmen, and young political leaders should be the primary target audiences. Once again, properly conceived exchange programs should be part of this mix.

If Europe and the Islamic world should be the top two priorities of American public diplomacy for the foreseeable future, this is by no means to suggest that the rest of the world may safely be ignored. China will remain of very considerable importance for American foreign policy in this century as it expands its economy, further develops a modern military establishment, and exerts its influence in more supple and effective ways not only in Asia but throughout the world.[38] American public diplomacy has already achieved a large audience base there,[39] and tens of thousands of Chinese students study in American universities every year. Chinese popular attitudes reflect a fund of goodwill toward the United States that is probably greater than in many other parts of the world, in spite of the rise of a new nationalism among the young and its deliberate fanning by the government (seen strikingly during the controversy over the shoot-down of an American EP-3 electronic surveillance aircraft near Hainan Island by a Chinese Air Force fighter in the spring of 2001). These advantages need to be preserved and exploited.

Russia has of course been a key target of American public diplomacy in the past, and may become so again in the future if its current slide toward authoritarianism continues. The constraints that are being increasingly imposed on the Russian press would seem to vindicate the argument some have made since the end of the Cold War that American surrogate broadcasting assets geared to the Soviet Union (Radio Liberty) should be retained as hedges against the potential failure of the democratic experiment in Russia or the other former Soviet republics. In any case, there have been a number of recent developments indicating the determination of the current Russian government to play a much more ambitious role in the soft power arena—notably, a new global English-language satellite television service, and (even more startling) a government-operated domestic television service focusing on military themes and geared to fostering patriotism.[40]

As for the rest of the world, it seems obvious that the United States should maintain balanced public diplomacy capabilities that provide relatively complete global coverage while at the same time permitting "surge" response to rapidly developing crises and unanticipated threats that may emerge over the longer term. Unfortunately, however, a diametrically opposite approach—one focused on immediate threats and the short term—has been the dominant one. Thus the recent public-relations style campaigns spearheaded by the then under secretary of State for Public Diplomacy and Public Affairs, Charlotte Beers, designed to show that Muslims in the United States are not hated or discriminated against, and the channeling of large U.S. government resources into new broadcasting ventures in the Arab world at the expense of long-established capabilities in places like Latin America. If we have learned one large lesson from the terror war, it is the essential unpredictability of our current strategic environment as well as its global nature. In any event, the "global reach" of contemporary Islamist terrorism means that we cannot afford to neglect any part of the globe, and particularly areas that have Muslim populations or a deficit of governance or some combination of both.

Africa is a prime candidate on both counts, and Al-Qaeda has already made its presence felt there (notably, in the bombings of U.S. embassies in Kenya and Tanzania in 1998). The U.S. military has over the last several years begun to build or expand its relationships with African governments and provide them counterterrorism aid and training. But the American diplomatic presence in Africa remains thin, and in other respects the reach of American soft power on the continent is extremely limited. Under these circumstances, a good case can be made that the United States (perhaps working with both European and local partners) should launch a major initiative to enhance technical communications capabilities throughout the region and work generally to enhance the access of ordinary Africans to news and ideas from the West.[41] Nor is it wise to neglect Latin America, at a time when democracy there may be faltering and Hugo Chavez, the Venezuelan strong man, has launched a virulent ideological and political challenge to the United States with potential cross-continental appeal.[42]

Identifying the two priority audiences of American public diplomacy today as Europe and the Islamic world has important implications, pointing as it does to a certain bifurcation in our strategic approach. One fundamental objective of our public diplomacy must be to help win the war on terror. A second fundamental objective, supporting this but also important in its own right and with its own requirements, is to enhance American global engagement and influence. These two objectives are not only distinct but in potential tension with one another. There can be little question that American diplomacy/public diplomacy has erred significantly over the last several years by its single-minded focus on the terror threat at the expense of this second objective. A perception has been widely fostered that the United States has overreacted to the terrorism problem, at the expense of long-standing relationships with allies and attention to other pressing international problems. This in turn has helped insinuate the idea that the United States is using the war on terror as a cover to make geopolitical gains or in other ways to advance a self-interested American agenda.[43]

Nowhere has this failure been more evident than in the by now received wisdom that the Bush administration acts "unilaterally" in the world with little or no regard for the views of its allies, the United Nations, or other interested parties. The administration has behaved for the most part as if it could simply ignore this charge and the resentment it has so clearly fanned in allied governments in Europe and in media and public opinion everywhere—thus seeming to confirm its truth. In fact, it is very largely false, and there is a great deal the administration could have said to refute it, or at least to provide mitigating explanations or arguments. It is difficult to overstate the impact on elite opinion in Europe and elsewhere of the apparently summary rejection by the Bush administration of the Kyoto Protocol on global warming, for example. In fact, as is well-known, Kyoto faced overwhelming opposition in the U.S. Congress and would never have been ratified there, and the United States had good reasons for its position, as well as some support for it from other countries (Australia and Russia also refused to ratify, though the latter soon changed its mind in return for a side payment from the Europeans). Yet nothing was done to soften the blow, and the result has been a public relations debacle of the first order. It can perhaps be argued that an extended public diplomacy effort on Kyoto by the United States would have been a waste of time given the level of irrationality in the public debate on environmental issues generally.[44] This is by no means so clear. But in any event, it is difficult to believe the United States could not have found it possible to be more demonstratively respectful of the political investment in Kyoto of most of the other advanced democracies, or to offer some constructive suggestions for the way ahead.

Over the last several years, it has become virtually a commonplace of public discourse in this country and abroad that the United States is or is in the process of becoming an "empire" or the chief organizer of a new global imperial order. Perhaps because "imperialist America" has for so long been a standard slur of left-wing propaganda, we seem to have difficulty taking this kind of talk seriously; but it is by no means now restricted to the Left.[45] There can be little question that it does manifest harm to the reputation of the U.S. overseas. Certainly, the U.S. government cannot control what American academics or journalists write or say, but it needs to be sensitive in its own public rhetoric to this toxic issue. More than that, it needs to develop a set of concepts and a vocabulary for discussing America's role in the contemporary world as part of a larger public diplomacy strategy to counter negative images of the United States and enhance American global influence in the longer term. Such a strategy should encompass a vision (building on the president's recent inaugural address) of the nature and limits of American support for democratization abroad, of the relationship of the United States to its friends and allies, and of the American role in the international political, legal, and economic orders. It should acknowledge the reality of American power while seeking to provide others reassurance as to ultimate American intentions as well as reasons to cooperate with rather than seeking to oppose the United States.[46]

CHAPTER 5

Problems of Legitimacy: The Cultural Context

It is not generally appreciated how profoundly American public diplomacy and strategic influence operations are shaped and constrained by American political culture. Paradoxical as it may seem, Americans cheerfully accept a constant barrage of commercial advertising that is often transparently manipulative and misleading and tolerate a great deal of skewered news reporting in the national media, yet remain very sensitive to any effort by the government to control the flow of information to them. This sensitivity is evident, for example, in the difficulties the U.S. government has long had in protecting classified information. Not only prior censorship but even post hoc prosecution of the media or former officials for disclosing even the most sensitive military or intelligence secrets is now virtually unthinkable in the United States, and the media have become accustomed—within certain limits—to retailing them.[1] The First Amendment, of course, has achieved iconic status within contemporary political discourse in the country, and this is true above all in the world of journalism, which for obvious reasons of institutional interest takes an even more absolutist view of the constitutional guarantee of freedom of speech than the general population.[2]

At first sight, it might seem that none of this should have any impact on information programs directed to audiences abroad. Yet as noted earlier, many of those who populate the public diplomacy agencies of the government are themselves professional journalists or tend to identify with the journalism profession. Such people model their own performance on the practice of the commercial media, and tend to see any interference with their supposed professional judgment as an illegitimate attempt at "censorship" by the government. At the same time, it would be naïve in the extreme to imagine that such attitudes reflect simply a quest for journalistic purity, and not a certain set of political or ideological views. Like most American journalists, many public diplomatists are political liberals. Over the last forty years or so, the trajectory of political liberalism has moved toward an increasingly dark view of the United States and its role in the world. This means that our public diplomatists or significant numbers of them are today no longer as convinced as they once were that America's story is after all fundamentally a good one, or believe an alternative, negative story is at least equally plausible. The consequences of this subterranean ideological shift have made themselves felt in many areas of public diplomacy over the last three decades or so. Above all, they have created pressures within public diplomacy organizations to distance those organizations as much as possible from the policy agencies of the U.S. government. These pressures have been particularly strong during periods of Republican ascendancy in Washington, beginning with the presidency of Richard Nixon. Moreover, they have been fanned by powerful allies in the Congress and the national media. Because of the absence of any domestic constituency for the output of public diplomacy organizations, and because most recent administrations have been unwilling to expend a great deal of political capital on such issues, these forces have had a disproportionate impact on the performance of the U.S. government in this area.

The Voice of America (VOA) is a prominent case in point. At VOA, the so-called "Charter" of this organization, enshrined in legislation in 1976, is regularly invoked against any attempts by external agencies such as the State Department—or even the radio's own editors and managers—to shape news coverage in ways not sanctioned by what is claimed to be professional journalistic judgment. There are three provisions of this document, which bear quoting in full: 1) "VOA will serve as a consistently reliable and authoritative source of news. VOA news will be accurate, objective, and comprehensive." 2) "VOA will represent America, not any single segment of American society, and will therefore present a balanced and comprehensive projection of significant American thought and institutions." 3) "VOA will present the policies of the United States clearly and effectively, and will also present responsible discussion and opinion on those policies."[3] It can be seen immediately that these provisions, for the most part perfectly reasonable, are also very general in nature and cannot possibly serve as anything like an operational code of conduct for the Voice of America. The intent of this language (which goes back to 1959) was simply to articulate the basic differences between American-style "public diplomacy" and Soviet-style "propaganda." Nothing on its face rules out an operational approach substantially different from that currently in effect in American commercial broadcasting, and certainly nothing mandates that *the* standard for interpreting this guidance must be sought in the commercial broadcasting world. What is striking, of course, is the utter absence in the Charter of any statement as to the fundamental purpose of the Voice. This has allowed advocates of an independent Voice to argue or assume that its purpose is not very different from the purpose of commercial broadcasting; yet there is little reason to suppose that any such idea was in the minds of the Charter's originators. The third provision enjoins VOA not only to present U.S. policy to the overseas audience, but to do it "effectively." This alone indicates that we are dealing with quite a different set of imperatives than is the case in commercial broadcasting.[4]

Illustrative of the deep misconceptions of VOA's role that have taken hold over the last several decades are several incidents that occurred shortly after the events of 9/11. In the first, VOA's Pashto service aired portions of an interview with Afghanistan's Taliban leader, Mullah Mohammed Omar, in which he commented on President Bush's speech to the nation on the terrorist attacks. The next day, a VOA reporter filed a story quoting remarks critical of the United States by the leader of the Egyptian organization Gama'a Islamiyya, which it failed to identify as a terrorist group associated with Al-Qaeda. When criticized for these egregious lapses, the news director of the Voice acknowledged the misrepresentation of Gama'a Islamiyya, but insisted that interviews with terrorists would continue to be "part of our balanced, accurate, objective and comprehensive reporting, providing our listeners with both sides of the story."[5]

Striking here is the invocation of the letter of the Charter in a way totally contrary to its spirit, conflating news reporting with commentary and ignoring the specific requirement to present U.S. policy "effectively" and to ensure that any discussion of that policy be "responsible." It can hardly be considered responsible to provide a platform for the opinions of a national leader with whom the United States would shortly be at war, or the head of a criminal terrorist organization. Our commercial media may see themselves under an obligation to "tell both sides of the story," in effect posturing themselves as a neutral observer between the United States and its enemies, though even this is by no means evident—especially after 9/11.[6] But it defies all reason to suppose that the Voice of America must adopt the role of a neutral observer, carefully "balancing" any positive presentation of the policies or actions of the government with negative reactions from hostile commentators, whether foreign leaders or for that matter home-grown pundits, politicians, or professors. The purpose of the Voice of America is, as its famous motto goes, to "tell America's story." It is not to provide others a platform for gratuitous criticism or contradiction of that story, even if their criticisms have some measure of merit—let alone to "balance," in effect, sense with nonsense. Newly installed VOA Director Robert Reilly put the matter perfectly in an internal memo circulated within hours of taking office: "We are in a war of ideas. We are on one side in that war. The other side presents the United States as the source of all evil in the world and contends, therefore, that it must be destroyed. One of the many differences that characterize our side in the war of ideas is that we are not afraid to tell the truth. Telling the truth requires a great deal more than simply recounting the positions of the various sides in a dispute. It requires an act of discernment as to the veracity of the contending claims."[7]

The flap over the Defense Department's Office of Strategic Influence (OSI) points to another—and related—fault line within the bureaucracies responsible for wartime information: the perennial tension between the mission of informing the domestic audience and the mission of managing dissemination of information abroad to serve the strategic goals of a war. The OSI was created shortly after the 9/11 attacks to develop a strategic approach and supporting programs to counter the appeal of radical Islamism within the Muslim world. Its director was Brigadier General Simon P. Worden, a respected Air Force officer and expert in information operations in the military sense of the term. As the title of the office suggested—and was meant to suggest—the scope of its activities exceeded public diplomacy as traditionally defined and involved a significant psychological operations and political warfare component. This included a (modest) covert element, primarily involving, it seems, influencing coverage of terrorism in the foreign press. Not surprisingly, in due course an article appeared in the *New York Times* claiming that the Pentagon was intent on providing "disinformation" to the press as part of its new strategic influence campaign.[8] Less surprising than the leak itself was that the allegations were not vigorously denied. It is now generally accepted that the reason for this was that the leak originated in DoD's own Office of Public Affairs, in a bureaucratic maneuver designed to discredit the OSI operation.[9]

The ensuing media firestorm seems to have caught the Pentagon leadership unprepared. In any event, after repeated denials that anyone in the Defense Department was planning to lie to the press, Secretary Rumsfeld threw in the towel and announced a week later that the OSI could no longer function effectively and would be shut down. A subsequent internal review of the matter by the Pentagon's general counsel later determined that no OSI document had actually proposed resorting to "disinformation" (or even used the word, except in the context of countering enemy efforts) or advocated lying to the press. The small proportion of its work that was to be done covertly involved the foreign press, and even here, there seems to be no indication that the actual materials to be provided were to convey anything other than truthful information. The great bulk of the proposed OSI programs were traditional public diplomacy and counterpropaganda. Some involved technical support for educational reform in Pakistan's *madrasas*—a program that reportedly had the enthusiastic support of Pakistani President Musharraf.[10] Moreover, contrary to the impression given in the press of a rogue operation, it seems that OSI's various initiatives had all been fully vetted and approved in interagency meetings with State Department public diplomacy officials.[11]

There are two lessons that emerge from this sorry spectacle. The first is the raw strength of the cultural animus against American "propaganda," particularly as exhibited in the prestige media (above all, the authoritative yet predictably liberal *New York Times* and *Washington Post*). The second is the difficulty senior government officials seem to have in grappling with the problem. Part of this can be traced to sheer ignorance. Yet a part has to do as well with the extent to which this cultural animus has itself penetrated the American national security bureaucracy and especially the public affairs elements of that bureaucracy, whose job it is to deal with the press on a day-to-day basis and protect their superiors from its periodic tantrums. Anyone who doubts that this problem is a persisting one should consider the recent media flap over U.S. military involvement in preparing news materials and paying for them to be run in the Iraqi press—a story leaked originally to the *Los Angeles Times* apparently by "military officials" who were unhappy with the practice.[12] In a media environment in which pro-American Iraqi journalists are at substantial physical risk, it is hardly outrageous for the United States not only to provide some compensation to them but to disguise its own role in doing so. In any event, the stories involved were apparently entirely truthful and intended to counter the misinformation and disinformation so rampant in the local media.[13]

It is sometimes imagined that the Reagan administration was able to effect a radical transformation in the culture and operating style of the national security bureaucracy in the public diplomacy arena. It is undeniable that the Reagan administration was committed to a more robust vision of public diplomacy than most career personnel in the public diplomacy agencies (or in the State Department) tended to be comfortable with, and also that a significant number of conservatives were brought into these organizations to attempt to implement that vision. And their track record of accomplishment was certainly substantial.[14] At the same time, however, they had to contend at all times with the constraining influence of the preexisting culture as well as the resistance of co-workers and subordinates who did not share their views. Indeed, they regularly found themselves under attack both from within and by liberals on Capitol Hill and in key congressional staffs and their allies in the press, on the grounds that their efforts to reinvigorate the practice of public diplomacy were "politicizing" otherwise professionally sound activities. It was argued, for example, that scrutiny by the new USIA leadership of the rolls of overseas speakers amounted to a "blacklist" of liberal academics and others previously used in this program.[15] The irony was that, with few exceptions, conservative speakers or ideas had been conspicuously absent from American public diplomacy efforts prior to Reagan.

The point here, however, is not that conservative ideas or ideology should dominate American public diplomacy, or even that they should be represented in programming according to some artificial standard of "balance." It is rather that American public diplomacy should never lose sight of its fundamental purpose, and that it should be judged by how effectively it carries out that purpose. This fundamental purpose is to influence the attitudes and behavior of foreign publics in ways that serve the national interests of the United States. If the canons of "political correctness" are to govern what the United States is allowed to say and do abroad, it is probably better simply to shut down the American public diplomacy apparatus and save the people's money.

It should go without saying that partisanship in the domestic political sense has no place in American public diplomacy. At the same time, however, the unhappy reality is that there is significant overlap between the views of many American liberals on important current policy questions facing the U.S. government and those of its critics abroad. This is true particularly of European elites—one of the highest priority targets of our public diplomacy today—as was argued earlier. It is impossible to defend American policies such as opposition to the Kyoto Protocol, or aspects of American life such as the pervasiveness of the death penalty, without at least some awareness of and openness to conservative arguments concerning these subjects. More generally, I would venture to suggest, there is a need for the United States to begin to educate the world about the nature of American conservatism. As effectively argued in a recent book by two English journalists,[16] conservatism is an increasingly important component of the American scene, and Europeans and others need to try to understand it if they are to understand why the United States behaves differently than other countries and in ways they find baffling or threatening. The demonizing of American "neo-conservatism" that we see in many parts of the world today (and for which American liberals themselves bear considerable responsibility), for example, is damaging to the nation as a whole; countering it in appropriate ways can be seen as a perfectly legitimate public diplomacy mission.

Stating the problem in these terms may seem a counsel of despair, and certainly no one should underestimate the difficulty of effecting change in political and organizational culture. Nevertheless, there are some obvious steps that might be taken. The various inadequacies in the VOA Charter and the gross misuse to which it has been subjected point to a more fundamental problem that affects every aspect of public diplomacy: the absence of "doctrine," to borrow again the military term of art. It is essential to clarify the roles and missions of U.S. international broadcasting and other public diplomacy entities, and to lay down operational guidelines concerning the nature and extent of policy control of these agencies' activities. It is unnecessary and would probably be politically unproductive to seek to replace the charter, but it should be supplemented by more detailed language and concrete procedures for ensuring the accountability of the VOA to policy authority, while at the same time protecting it from unwarranted day-to-day interference in its operations. Some suggestions along these lines will be made later on. The same point applies to sorting out the problematic relationship between public affairs and psychological-political warfare within the defense establishment.

Beyond all this, however, what is needed is a sustained and honest national debate on these issues that seeks to develop a new political consensus on the role of strategic influence broadly understood in the contemporary security environment. That there has been a serious loss of perspective on these matters is evident. Without in any way denying that there are real questions concerning the scope of what the government should be permitted to do in this arena, I believe the main burden lies with liberal critics, who continue to use these issues largely as ways to score ideological points and show little evidence of making any serious effort to come to grips with them intellectually or to develop constructive alternative ideas. It is heartening that many of the studies and reports on public diplomacy of the last few years have had at least a flavor of bipartisanship; the problem is that they have tended to shy away from issues perceived as ideologically divisive. In the past, Congress has sometimes played a constructive role in this regard. Unfortunately, there is little interest in or understanding of public diplomacy in Congress today, and as we shall see, the Senate has been a major factor in the wrong turn taken in recent years by U.S. international broadcasting. Perhaps the time has come to have a high-level commission (jointly appointed perhaps by the president and Congress) address the subject, as was last done in the 1970s by the so-called "Stanton Commission." With that thought in mind, we turn to the related yet distinct set of problems involved in the organization of public diplomacy and strategic influence operations within the U.S. government.

CHAPTER 6

Problems of Organization: The Bureaucratic Context

Since the outbreak of World War II, there has probably been more instability in the strategic communications sector of the American national security bureaucracy than in any other. During the war itself, long-running and bitter disputes over roles and missions marked relations between the three organizations with responsibilities in this area, the Office of War Information, the Office of Strategic Services (forerunner of the CIA), and the psychological warfare branch of the Army.[1] A residual information service was kept after the war as a semi-autonomous bureau of the State Department, but the Voice of America came close to being abolished. With the outbreak of the Korean War, interest in public diplomacy revived within the Truman administration and in Congress, but there was little consensus on how it should be organized. In 1953, after much internal study, the United States Information Agency was created by President Dwight D. Eisenhower, but largely because of the reluctance of Secretary of State Dulles to have his department run what he saw as an operational or programmatic function. The Voice of America joined the new agency, but the education and cultural affairs function was rather illogically retained by State. Meanwhile, the newly formed CIA had set out to create its own broadcasting empire with the creation of

Radio Free Europe (1950) and Radio Liberty (1953) as "surrogate" radios targeted at Eastern Europe and the Soviet Union respectively, and in addition sponsored an array of political action campaigns directed against the growing threat of Soviet communism.[2] Meanwhile, the military too maintained a foothold in this arena, though its psychological warfare capabilities had declined greatly from their wartime heights.[3]

The involvement in public diplomacy and influence operations of a variety of very different and potentially competing organizations raised the question of coordination, and hence in particular the question of the White House role. As a Defense Department official lamented at the time, "Our psychological operating agencies are like bodies of troops without a commander and staff. Not having been told what to do or where to go, but too dynamic to stand still, the troops have marched in all directions."[4] In response to the Korean War, the Truman administration created a "Psychological Strategy Board" under the auspices of the recently established National Security Council (NSC) to organize and spearhead this effort, but it was able to make only limited headway, and was abolished near the beginning of the Eisenhower administration. The reorganized NSC system of the Eisenhower years included an "Operations Coordinating Board" that was assigned public diplomacy and related tools as part of its responsibility for interagency coordination of the implementation of foreign and national security policy generally, but its public diplomacy focus seems gradually to have dissipated. Only in the Reagan administration was an effort later made to reestablish an interagency coordinating mechanism for public diplomacy under NSC auspices, but again with only limited success.

The 1970s again saw major organizational change. Following the exposure of the CIA connection to Radio Free Europe and Radio Liberty on the floor of the U.S. Senate in 1971 and the resulting threat to the radios' continued existence, a new oversight mechanism, the presidentially appointed Board for International Broadcasting (BIB), was created by Congress in 1973. In 1976, the two radios and their respective corporate boards were merged into a single entity, "RFE-RL." Then it was the turn of USIA.[5] In 1977, in the wake of a number of outside studies of the organization of the foreign affairs agencies of the government,[6] the Carter administration decided to merge the State Department's Bureau of Education and Cultural Affairs (ECA) into USIA, while also changing the name of the parent agency to the U.S. International Communications Agency. At the same time, the administration also promulgated a new mission statement for the agency. It was enjoined as usual to let other nations and peoples "know where this great country stands, and why," yet it also claimed that "it is in our interest—and in the interest of other nations—that Americans have the opportunity to understand the histories, cultures, and problems of others, so that we can come to understand their hopes, perceptions and aspirations."[7] This so-called second mandate was a startling innovation that seemed to turn on its head the entire purpose of public diplomacy and to call for the establishment of an altogether new bureaucratic entity to carry it out. In practice, the second mandate never amounted to anything. But the episode is revealing, for it underlined the extent to which public diplomacy at this time seemed to be losing fundamental legitimacy even in the eyes of its own practitioners.

In the most influential of the studies just mentioned, the report of the so-called "Stanton Commission,"[8] several recommendations were made which, though not adopted at the time, would shape in important ways the future course of the debate on these issues. Going back to fundamentals, the Stanton Commission identified the core missions of public diplomacy as follows: exchange of persons, general information, policy information, and policy advice. (By "policy advice," it meant the shaping of policy decisions by public diplomacy considerations, as advocated by Murrow among others.) It then pinpointed as the key problem "the assignment, to an agency separate from and independent of the State Department, of the task of interpreting U.S. foreign policy and advising in its formulation." It also noted "the ambiguous positioning of the Voice of America at the crossroads of journalism and diplomacy." This analysis led the commission to the findings that 1) USIA should be abolished and replaced with a new, quasi-independent "Information and Cultural Affairs Agency" which would "combine the cultural and 'general information' programs' of both USIA and State's ECA bureau," 2) State should establish a new "Office of Policy Information, headed by a deputy under secretary, to administer all programs which articulate and explain U.S. foreign policy," and 3) the Voice of America should be set up as an independent federal agency under its own board of overseers.

These Stanton Commission recommendations responded to two very different if not contradictory requirements. The first was a perceived need to enhance the "credibility" of American public diplomacy by increasing its distance from the government; this acknowledged the eroding legitimacy of public diplomacy in the 1970s that was noted a moment ago. The second was to fix what the Commission saw as an artificial and ultimately dysfunctional organizational separation between the State Department, the agency responsible for formulating U.S. policy, and USIA insofar as it was responsible for defending U.S. policy and disseminating it abroad. In a sense, this reform too was intended to enhance the credibility of U.S. overseas information programs, but it would do so by narrowing their distance from government policy, not increasing it. Henceforth, the State Department would speak for itself—and thereby necessarily assume greater responsibility for the accuracy, timeliness, and effectiveness of its information efforts.

As it turned out, the next stage of public diplomacy reorganization in the mid-1990s, culminating in the merger of USIA with the State Department in 1998, largely embraced the Stanton Commission approach. Though its vision for USIA itself was not realized, the information functions of the old USIA were indeed folded into State, while the Congress created a new position of under secretary for Public Diplomacy and Public Affairs in the State Department designed to give public diplomacy new visibility and clout there. At the same time, significant steps were being taken toward autonomy for U.S. international broadcasters. Under the International Broadcasting Act of 1994, a new oversight board, the Broadcasting Board of Governors (BBG), replaced the Board for International Broadcasting, and was assigned authority not only over RFE-RL and the more recently created surrogate radios (Radio Marti and Radio Free Asia), but over the Voice of America itself. Though situated initially within USIA, the BBG was given in its authorizing legislation virtual operational control of all of U.S. international broadcasting. It is certainly true that VOA had enjoyed much de facto autonomy when it reported to USIA; and it needs to be noted that the secretary of State was made an ex officio member of the BBG. Nevertheless, the stage was now set for the eventual liberation of all U.S. overseas broadcasting from U.S. government control. And it soon became clear that this was indeed the direction the newly empowered BBG intended to take it in.

In the 1980s, the Reagan administration revitalized and empowered USIA and the surrogate radios, and yet at the same time thought it necessary to anchor public diplomacy more firmly in the White House and within the National Security Council system than had been the case since the 1950s. National Security Decision Directive (NSDD) 77, signed by the president in 1982, created a high-level Special Planning Group (SPG) for Public Diplomacy (the National

Security Adviser himself was the nominal chair) supported by interagency committees for international information (USIA chair), international political activities (State chair), international broadcasting (NSC chair), and "public affairs" (cochaired by NSC and the White House Office of Communications).[9] Perceptions differ as to the effectiveness of this arrangement.[10] The SPG itself very rarely met. The other committees, nominally chaired at the under secretary level, devolved relatively quickly to others; while their activity level was high initially, it tended to taper off as initiatives were adopted and programs established in the agencies. The International Broadcasting Committee was kept busy owing largely to the administration's ambitious radio modernization effort, which necessitated much diplomatic activity with host countries; and it also pushed a technical agenda focusing on countering Soviet jamming of U.S. radio signals. Only the Public Affairs Committee, focusing as it did on day-to-day communications strategy geared primarily toward the domestic media, approached a truly institutionalized status, but the precise connection between these activities and "public diplomacy" proper was never made particularly clear. In the second Reagan term, as a new spirit of cooperation with the reforming Soviet leadership under Mikhail Gorbachev began to take hold, much of the impetus behind the original public diplomacy effort slackened, and the Iran-Contra scandal dampened any appetite in the White House for a role in public diplomacy that looked in any way "operational." The SPG and associated structures were formally abolished in 1987.

The White House attitude toward public diplomacy thereafter remained for the most part passive and aloof until 9/11. Late in the Clinton administration, the president signed a directive on "International Public Information" intended to give the White House a role in coordination of public affairs, public diplomacy, and psychological operations; but this quickly devolved to the State Department.[11] As American military action in Afghanistan began to unfold in the fall of 2001, it became apparent that some special effort was needed to counter the propaganda operations of the Taliban regime and in general to prepare the information battlefield for the coming conflict both internationally and in Afghanistan itself, especially once it became apparent that the uniformed military could not exercise interagency leadership in this area.[12] What resulted was a combined U.S.-U.K. initiative establishing so-called "Coalition Information Centers (CICs)" in Washington, London, and Islamabad, Pakistan (designed to provide continuous twenty-four-hour coverage of the global news cycle), working directly for the American and British heads of state. Eventually, the Washington CIC evolved into what appears to have become a permanent office in the White House, the Office of Global Communications (OGC, formally created in March 2003). This office conducts daily conference calls with public affairs officials throughout the national security agencies, and publishes on a daily basis guidance documents with themes and messages for use in American posts overseas.[13] Meanwhile, in September 2002 a Policy Coordinating Committee (PCC) on Strategic Communications had been established within the National Security Council system, co-chaired by the under secretary of State for Public Affairs and Public Diplomacy (then Charlotte Beers) and a senior NSC staffer. On paper, at any rate, this combination of a high-level policy coordinating group directly anchored in the White House with a White House-centered operational public diplomacy staff seemed a reasonable answer to the new requirements of the global war on terror.

In fact, however, there was less to all this than met the eye. Charlotte Beers left the State Department in March 2003, and the PCC did not meet for more than a year. Another PCC, on "Muslim World Outreach," was also theoretically established in 2003 but has accomplished little. As for the OGC, by all accounts it has been fully captured by the White House public relations imperatives mentioned above—short-term, reactive, oriented to the domestic media, and pre-sidentially centered. The Coalition Information Centers in Pakistan and Afghanistan were closed in 2003, and the White House vetoed the idea of creating a new one in Iraq. Nor has the OGC made any real effort to coordinate public diplomacy efforts across agencies, and indeed, lacks a real interest in public diplomacy at all in the sense of a proactive and strategic instrument in the war on terror.[14] In recognition of these problems and of growing public criticism, the White House in early 2005 announced a reorganization of the NSC staff creating five new "deputy national security advisers," of which one would be assigned to "strategic communications and global outreach" and another to "global democracy strategy."[15] It is as yet unclear what impact this new arrangement will have.

Finally, some mention should be made of the more peripheral bureaucratic players in this arena. As mentioned earlier, the Central Intelligence Agency has in the past played a very significant role in psychological-political warfare. It created and managed into the 1970s the "gray propaganda" stations Radio Free Europe and Radio Liberty, engaged periodically in "black propaganda" radio operations and press placements, and undertook a variety of political action missions. The public record is unclear as to how much of this still goes on.[16] There can be little question in any case that major problems have been encountered over the years in integrating these kinds of activities into larger strategic influence operations, given their sensitive character and—more than that—the secretive and unilateralist culture of the CIA. If anything, this situation has been made worse by the intelligence legislation of the 1970s mandating special procedures for the handling and approval of "covert action" by the president and Congress. The existence of these cumbersome procedures has also undoubtedly been a major reason for the dwindling interest and capacity of the CIA in psychological-political warfare.[17]

None of this is to suggest that this development is necessarily to be regretted. There is little reason to think that RFE-RL has been any the worse off for severing its relationship to the agency (which was tenuous in any event). In the political action area, there have clearly been substantial advantages in moving these activities from the shadows into the open, a process initiated by the Reagan administration's "Project Democracy" and eventually institutionalized in the form of the National Endowment for Democracy (NED) and its affiliated organizations, especially the International Democratic Institute and the International Republican Institute. The quasi-private character of these organizations allows them to replicate the so-called "deniability" of covert operations while at the same time enhancing the credibility of the programs being supported. At the same time, the problems of integration and coordination with overall government policy certainly persist, and in some respects may have worsened. NED, the State Department, and the Agency for International Development (AID) are now all in the business of running programs in the areas of education reform, political reform, state-building, civil society, and democratization, while interagency mechanisms for coordinating these programs remain weak or non-existent.

As regards AID, though nominally answerable to the authority of the secretary of state, its operational culture is very different from that of the State Department and both agencies have traditionally kept a distance from one another. There has been some improvement in this situation under the leadership of recently departed AID director Andrew Natsios. However, there is general recognition that major organizational reforms in this area are needed. Very recently, Secretary of State Condoleezza Rice has announced, as part of a larger reform program she calls "transformational diplomacy," that the director of AID will henceforth operate out of the State Department itself and be "dual-hatted" as coordinator of all foreign assistance programs administered by state.[18]

This abbreviated history is essential background as one tries to come to grips with the various deficiencies of American public diplomacy and strategic influence operations today. We will now look in greater detail at each of the major organizations or organizational arenas just discussed, analyzing the critical problems that currently hamper their effectiveness and what could be done to address them.

CHAPTER 7

The State Department: Back to the Future?

There is a great deal to be said in favor of the view taken by the Stanton Commission that the same agency that is responsible for the formulation of U.S. foreign policy should also be responsible for making that policy generally known and for explaining and defending it. Diplomats can make excellent propagandists, and substantive policy experts will always have more credibility than those seen as mere flacks. Moreover, tightening organizational links between policymakers and public diplomatists would seem to result in many administrative efficiencies. It was also eminently plausible to suppose that once handed this mission of the former USIA, as well as many of the people and resources that had been committed to it, the State Department would embrace these responsibilities, support them appropriately, and carry them out effectively. Unfortunately, the reality has been far otherwise.

Allowance of course has to be made for the inevitable confusion and inefficiencies of any major reorganization. Yet it is now some five years since the State-USIA merger, and there is still no sign that the State Department has either the vision or the will to conduct effective public diplomacy. Fundamental problems remain at the level of organizational structure, culture, and leadership.

The public diplomacy structure of the State Department following the merger centers on the office of International Information Programs (IIP) and the Educational and Cultural Affairs (ECA) bureau—both formerly part of USIA—under the under secretary for Public Diplomacy and Public Affairs. In addition, public diplomacy officers in modest numbers are seeded throughout State's regional bureaus, the core policy-formulating element of the department, and are assigned to U.S. embassies overseas. Another important component of the former USIA, the Office of Media Research and Analysis, is attached to the bureau of Intelligence and Research (INR). Finally, mention should be made of the Bureau of Democracy, Human Rights, and Labor, currently reporting to the under secretary for Global Affairs. While the activities of this bureau certainly involve elements of traditional diplomacy, many also fall into the information or political action categories and hence might seem more properly to belong to the domain of public diplomacy.

The key problem is that the under secretary has no authority over the public diplomacy functions or personnel not in his or her direct chain of command, and also has little say over resource issues relating to public diplomacy. Personnel matters affecting public diplomacy officers in the field are handled by the ambassador, not at the Washington level, as in the past. In addition, senior public diplomacy officers in the regional bureaus are too few and at too low a level (office directors rather than deputy assistant secretaries) to ensure real integration with policymaking, and have tended to become isolated.

But the more fundamental problem is that of organizational culture. As one public diplomacy officer remarked of the merger, USIA people "have come from an organization that sent out information and arrived in an organization that draws information in and by nature keeps it locked in."[1] The information function has always lacked prestige within the culture of the Foreign Service, and is currently ghettoized (that is, public diplomacy is a fifth career "cone" within the Foreign Service, distinct from the prestigious political cone). This has meant consistent undermanning and underfunding of public diplomacy activities. State provides inadequate training in the discipline for public diplomacy officers, not to speak of its other personnel. Moreover, the highly bureaucratic character of the State Department, with its elaborate and time-consuming system of clearances and paperwork, is antithetical to the requirements of effective public diplomacy, which must be sensitive to news cycles and capable of responding immediately in crisis situations. USIA, by contrast, was programmatically-oriented, capable of producing tangible products quickly and efficiently. Finally, with few exceptions, the Foreign Service tends to lack an appreciation of the real nature of public diplomacy, and in fact, to confuse it with public affairs. It sees public diplomacy as fundamentally reactive rather than proactive. Its attitude toward releasing information is to "fire and forget"; it is not accustomed to run extended information campaigns carefully calculated to produce certain effects on certain audiences. And it favors blandness and banality over argumentation, controversy, and color.[2]

Finally, the State Department has failed to provide the leadership so clearly needed to overcome these deficiencies. Under the Clinton administration, little high-level attention was paid to any of these issues during the crucial reorganization period, while in the Bush administration, a critical mistake was made in appointing to the position of under secretary for Public Diplomacy and Public Affairs an advertising executive without foreign policy expertise or Washington experience, Charlotte Beers, who led the department down the blind alley of "branding" the United States as a Muslim-friendly society. Nor did Secretary Powell take any apparent interest in this subject.[3] Following Beers' departure in March 2003, the position was left vacant for nine months; the eventual successor, Margaret Tutwiler, previously ambassador to Morocco and apparently a reluctant volunteer, left after only a brief tenure.

It is conceivable that stronger leadership at the political level could effect changes in State Department culture that, over the longer term at least, would enable it to perform the public diplomacy mission satisfactorily. Yet one cannot but be deeply pessimistic at the prospects for this, given the widespread view in Washington today—voiced most forcefully several years ago by former House speaker Newt Gingrich, but echoed as well within the ranks of the Foreign Service itself—that the State Department as a whole has not risen to the challenges of the contemporary era.[4] This is a large issue beyond the scope of the present discussion. But to cite only one problem relevant to our concerns, the complete failure of the department to create incentives or a career structure encouraging higher education in its officers (comparable, for example, to the uniformed military) has led to a situation of acute deficit in knowledge of languages, culture and history throughout the Foreign Service.[5] To be sure, the fault cannot be laid entirely at the feet of the department, as Congress—for unfathomable reasons—has for many years regularly denied State even minimally adequate funding and personnel levels.

The obvious question, then, is whether the State-USIA merger was a mistake and ought to be reversed. The critics of American public diplomacy today are divided on this issue, though most tend to regard the question as all but moot as a practical matter (also the apparent position of the Bush administration). It will be argued here that the merger was probably an experiment worth trying,[6] but one that has signally failed. It is simply unrealistic to look to the State Department to undertake the full range of public diplomacy activities, to do so aggressively and creatively, or to run "programs" in an efficient and responsive way—either now or in any foreseeable future. Therefore, I shall argue, "USIA" will continue to be needed and should be reinvented.[7] At the same time, both on the merits and for sound practical reasons, it would be wrong to try to undo everything that has been done to improve the integration of public diplomacy and policy at the State Department. On the contrary, I believe it is essential to continue to press state to do more and better in this area. And if USIA is to be reconstituted, it is also an open question whether it should be reconstituted in its earlier form. What needs to be done, then, is to provide a plan for redefining the role of public diplomacy at the State Department as well as for reviving USIA in a way that suits contemporary requirements.

The Stanton Commission was broadly correct to recommend that State should take over only those USIA functions that directly involve policy information and advice, and that USIA should have the cultural function (and the ECA bureau). It was wrong, however, in attempting to exclude USIA from any policy-related role, limiting it essentially to educational and cultural affairs and to "general information" about America and American society in a longer-term perspective. The real question is how to sort out the exact division of labor between state and USIA relative to policy-related information, and, we may here add, *action*, an aspect of public diplomacy the Commission failed completely to address.

The fallacy of a sharp separation between educational and cultural affairs and "policy" is if anything even clearer today than it was in the 1970s. In the context of a conflict which is not merely ideological in nature but (in some sense at least) a "clash of civilizations," in Samuel Huntington's now classic phrase, education and culture are front and center in a way they were not during the Cold War. Hence the idea that education and culture represent an arena for essentially nonpolitical interaction with adversaries simply cannot be sustained today, and it becomes difficult to see what advantage is gained from assigning a separate organization to oversee that arena. This is by no means to argue that educational and cultural public diplomacy must in all cases be carried out by a government agency; indeed, there may be very great advantages in giving the private sector the lead in many of them. It is only to argue that there is a compelling argument for retaining at least some policy control over these activities.[8]

What public diplomacy-relevant tasks can be performed only or most effectively out of the State Department? There seem to be two, closely related but distinct: ensuring the closest possible connectivity between public diplomacy and diplomacy or policy, and exploiting the synergy between public diplomacy and policy. If this is correct, it suggests a clear standard for judging the sorts of public diplomacy activities that are appropriate for State and those that are not, and at the same time it underlines the importance of fixing some of the organizational problems noted a moment ago. Connectivity requires day-to-day collaboration between policy and public diplomacy officers to ensure that the public diplomacy implications of evolving policies are thoroughly understood, that policy itself is shaped by public diplomacy considerations as appropriate, that policy is articulated in a way that takes full account of its public impact abroad, and finally, that policy is supported in the process of implementation by supplementary information and materials that help explain and defend it (background documents, briefing slides, talking points, "Q&As," and the like). This kind of day-to-day collaboration clearly has its operational side, but these are not operational activities that can be easily reduced to a "program" to be executed elsewhere; they are (or must be if they are to be effective) inextricably enmeshed in the routine work of the department.

Ensuring this connectivity then makes it possible to exploit the synergy between public diplomacy and diplomacy. As noted earlier, this is a neglected but nonetheless important dimension of our subject. Diplomacy can support and reinforce public diplomacy campaigns, lending valuable credibility to messages that might otherwise be dismissed by foreign governments or other observers as mere propaganda. And public diplomacy can support diplomacy by bringing pressure to bear on foreign governments through their own media and public opinion. Further, diplomats may engage directly in public diplomacy campaigns, that is, in face-to-face interactions with various non-governmental foreign audiences; this is an important part of what we have referred to as the political action component of public diplomacy. Obviously, all of these things can only occur in and through the State Department.

The organizational implications of all this for the State Department are reasonably clear. Public diplomacy must avoid ghettoization by having a presence in each regional bureau and also in the functional bureaus (currently very uneven and in some cases non-existent). This presence should be at a sufficiently high level to ensure that the collaboration we have spoken about actually takes place, and that means at the level of deputy assistant secretary (at least in the regional bureaus). Further, the under secretary for Public Diplomacy and Public Affairs should be given clear administrative authority over these public diplomacy officers in the regional and functional bureaus (though for operational purposes they would of course answer to their respective assistant secretaries). This is almost certainly the only way to ensure that the integrity of the public diplomacy function is respected throughout the department. It appears that this change is in fact now occurring under the leadership of the new Under Secretary, Karen Hughes.[9]

At the same time, under this plan the under secretary would lose the two "programmatic" bureaus currently under his or her direct control (ECA and IIP) to a reconstituted USIA, while a new, relatively lean bureau would need to be created—perhaps called simply the Public Diplomacy bureau—to perform functions essential to the core State Department public diplomacy mission. In addition to supporting the under secretary's new administrative responsibilities, this bureau should include a public diplomacy policy planning and resources element and a crisis response element with a small operations center.[10] It would presumably have some regionally oriented structure, but should also have sufficient staff to allow flexible task organization to deal with emerging issues and to play effectively in the interagency arena.

A number of recent studies have urged the upgrading of IIP from an office to a bureau, headed by an assistant secretary, to increase the clout of public diplomacy within the department. With various of its current operational functions stripped away, as suggested here, some may doubt whether there could be sufficient justification for a new Public Diplomacy bureau, or indeed whether a new entity would be needed at all. Given the enormous daily volume of information and the constant ebbs and flows in U.S. policy, however, it is difficult to imagine that such a staff would not have enough to do. Moreover, an assistant secretary is a valuable asset not only in keeping public diplomacy visible and attended to throughout the department, but also in representing State effectively in the interagency arena and indeed abroad. There is plainly much work to be done in our diplomatic dealings with friends and allies abroad to raise awareness of public diplomacy as a strategic tool and to enlist them in multilateral public diplomacy initiatives of all kinds.[11] Let us also note that such a staff should be expected to play a key role in maintaining connectivity and coordination with state's very important Public Affairs bureau, which also answers to the under secretary.

Finally, there is the question of the proper locus in the State Department of what we have called "political action," and more generally, the relationship between the responsibilities of the under secretary for Public Diplomacy and Public Affairs and State's activities in the area of democratization and human rights. It can certainly be argued that the Bureau of Democracy, Human Rights, and Labor is a more natural fit for the public diplomacy under secretary than for the under secretary for Global Affairs (recently renamed under secretary for Democracy and Global Affairs), whose span of control currently includes in addition the Bureau of Oceans and International Environmental and Scientific Affairs and the Bureau of Population, Refugees and Migration.[12] At the same time, a case could be made for enlarging the Democracy bureau to cover a wider range of traditional political action functions. There is already a separate office for International Women's Issues under the Global Affairs under secretary; this is a subject of great salience for American public diplomacy in the Muslim world, and would be an obvious candidate for bringing into closer proximity to State public diplomacy. In addition, new offices could be created for issues relating to youth, religion, sports, and perhaps other such sectors of high significance in international public opinion.

It is predictable that relocation and reconfiguration of the Democracy bureau in the manner suggested here would be widely resisted within the department and perhaps beyond, on the grounds that promotion of democracy and human rights is part of the substance of American foreign policy and would be fatally undercut in the minds of its beneficiaries by association with (non-substantive) public diplomacy. The counterargument is that it is impossible to separate what we as a government say about these matters from what we do about them. I believe that both the public diplomacy and the democracy promotion sides of this equation would benefit from such an arrangement.[13] What it would provide in effect, for the first time, is a single institutional focal point within the government for American "soft power." Such a change would of course raise many questions. Whether the Public Diplomacy under secretary position would retain its current title is an obvious one. A case could certainly be made for changing it, but terminology in this entire area remains a vexing problem.

Where then does all this leave USIA? The general principle I have been trying to establish is that a revived USIA should no longer have a substantial role in generating and managing day-to-day or routine "policy information," as it did prior to the merger; this properly belongs with State. But it would retain a number of important roles relating to policy information. Several additional general principles may now be introduced to help define the scope and nature of USIA's activities.

First, USIA should again be seen as *the* institutional base of public diplomacy in the U.S. government. This should be understood to include broad responsibility for training and career development as well as the guardianship of what we have called public diplomacy "doctrine," something that has been done inadequately if at all in the past. It also implies the reintegration of international broadcasting in the agency, as will be discussed shortly. Second, USIA should be the primary operational agency for public diplomacy. Though State's operational role would be recognized and accommodated, USIA would regain responsibility for managing public diplomacy operations in the field, including jurisdiction over the Public Affairs Officers in the embassies.[14] It would also regain ownership of the Media Research and Analysis unit currently in State/INR and the Foreign Press Centers. (By contrast, it would make sense to have the Washington ("Wireless") File, a daily compilation of government-generated information distributed electronically to U.S. embassies around the world and heavily used, remain at the State Department.) Moreover, USIA rather than State would have the lead role in developing and fielding new technological capabilities in support of public diplomacy— perhaps in a new and closer relationship with the Department of Defense.

USIA's role under this scheme should not be seen as only operational or programmatic. It would have the lead responsibility for research and analysis relative to the foreign media and foreign public opinion, and, along with the State Department, would engage in strategic planning relative to public diplomacy campaigns and programs. Like State, it would generate policy-relevant information, but its activities would be more proactive and creative. Its products might range from formal "white papers," to primers on American foreign policy or the American political system geared to a variety of foreign audiences, to the production of documentary films or TV features on policy issues such as global warming or on contemporary history. A major function (though one that would need to be shared to some degree with State, Defense, and the Intelligence Community) would be the monitoring, analysis, exposure, and countering of adversary propaganda and disinformation activities—an occasional USIA function in the past, mostly in wartime, but now arguably required on a sustained basis. And as it has in the past, USIA should administer speakers programs abroad addressing policy issues; and its field officers should engage continuously on these issues with foreign journalists, academics, and other opinion-makers. It should attempt to revive its former network of American libraries oversees, and oversee major new programs to disseminate books and written materials of all kinds to key foreign audiences. Finally, USIA should facilitate contacts between high-ranking American officials throughout the government and key influentials and audiences abroad, something that has never been done very systematically in the past.

This last point is an important one, as it underlines one of the great advantages of having a USIA separate from the State Department. USIA should be seen as serving U.S. foreign policy in the largest sense, not simply American diplomacy; it should work cooperatively with every agency of the U.S. government that has significant overseas presence or interests—the Agency for International Development as well as the departments of Energy, Commerce, Agriculture, Justice, and (particularly) Defense. This raises, however, a perennial issue: whether USIA should be formally subordinated to the authority of the secretary of State, as in the past, or rather become a fully independent organization with its own recognized place at the pinnacle of the national security apparatus and a direct relationship with the president. This question cannot be resolved without looking more broadly at the current interagency system and how it might be reformed in order to foster a more coherent approach to American soft power generally—an issue to which I shall return later.

The USIA envisioned here would retain much of the programmatic orientation of the old USIA, as just indicated. Where it could improve on its predecessor organization is in having greater agility and flexibility, a higher level of creative and analytic capability, and greater engagement in the substance of the issues with which public diplomacy deals. In these respects, it would hark back in significant ways to an older model, the Office of War Information of World War II vintage, which was staffed by a very distinguished group of journalists and intellectuals.[15] To build such an organization, however, would require quite a different approach to personnel recruitment and retention than what existed at the old USIA or prevails currently at the State Department. While some number of career civil and Foreign Service personnel will always be desirable in such an agency, ways need to be found as well to bring in talented non-career people for limited tours. These could be new PhDs in a variety of relevant fields, they could be mid-career businessmen with significant foreign experience and language skills, or they could even be early retirees, particularly former military officers. Some could perhaps be hired on a contract basis rather than as regular government employees. Preserving flexibility in firing as well as hiring should be a consideration in any case, given the high potential for burnout in many of these jobs. For whatever reason, the two organizations in the U.S. government today whose employees are on average the oldest are the Voice of America and the International Information Programs bureau of the State Department.[16] This situation simply has to be corrected if we are to be serious about public diplomacy.

Recently, a study sponsored by the Defense Science Board has made a forceful case for creating a "Center for Strategic Communications" that would have roughly the status of a Federally Funded Research and Development Center (FFRDC) with its own corporate board, like the RAND Corporation.[17] Though the study does not draw the connection, its description of the functions and activities of such a center is not very different from the one offered here of a USIA remade to be more lean, agile, analytical, and creative than its predecessor. It is far from clear just what advantages such a center would have over a government agency other than greater flexibility in the personnel field, since it would probably be perceived as virtually part of the government and would be constrained by various government regulations; but it would surely raise serious issues of control and accountability. In fact, it would invite a replay of the very unsatisfactory state of affairs currently existing in the international broadcasting arena, to which we now turn.

CHAPTER 8

International Broadcasting: Who's in Charge?

Since the end of the Cold War, there has been a major revolution in the governance structure of U.S. international broadcasting which has had little-noticed but potentially far-reaching consequences. In 1994, the United States International Broadcasting Act[1] consolidated all U.S.-sponsored radio and television broadcasting under the Broadcasting Board of Governors (BBG), a part-time, bipartisan board of eight presidentially appointed individuals from the private sector, with the Secretary of State as an ex officio member. The BBG was to be supported by an International Broadcasting Bureau (IBB), a federal entity that provides technical and support services for all U.S. broadcasters and directly controls the Voice of America and Radio/TV Marti[2] as well as the television capabilities of the former USIA. The former "surrogate" radios, Radio Free Europe/Radio Liberty and Radio Free Asia, while also under the overall authority of the BBG, would retain their ambiguous status as private but nevertheless entirely government-funded "grantees" of the board.

On paper, at least at first sight, this arrangement might seem to entail an actual strengthening of U.S. government control of international broadcasting. Unlike the old Board for International Broadcasting, the oversight mechanism for the surrogate radios after

1975, the BBG was given unambiguous legislative authority to "direct and supervise" all non-military broadcasting activities of the government; the Secretary of State was placed on the board itself and invited or required to provide "information and guidance on foreign policy issues," and the Board itself reported to USIA. Under these circumstances, one might have thought that USIA and State would seize the opportunity and take a more aggressive role in ensuring that all U.S. broadcasters reflect the foreign policy priorities of the administration and the nation. At the very least, it might have asserted a right, on the basis of the secretary's ex officio role if nothing else, to veto certain kinds of decisions.

In fact, few expected this would happen, and it did not happen. The letter of the International Broadcasting Act may have left some room for such a role by USIA and State, but its spirit was the spirit of the Stanton Commission, with its fundamental discomfort over government control of broadcasting. In a striking departure from the past, the Act actually vested in the BBG the power to make decisions concerning the creation, alteration, or abolition of language services, something that had always been regarded as a policy matter over which the State Department and the White House would have the final say.[3] And the political environment in which the Act was adopted only further reinforced such tendencies. The Clinton administration cared little for public diplomacy. The State Department was not interested in asserting any role for itself in the broadcasting arena, and USIA, in spite of some attempts to resist the tide, remained on the sidelines. But the key development was the early capture of the BBG by individuals with powerful ties both to the domestic broadcasting industry and to the Democratic Party who were committed to pursuing aggressively an agenda of de facto privatization of U.S. international broadcasting. Under their impact, the Board was able gradually to establish itself not indeed as an advisory board to the State Department or the White House, but as the de facto operational authority for all U.S. government broadcasting.[4] The advent of the Bush administration in 2001 has done nothing to change this situation. In fact, because it has offered the Board the apparent imprimatur of a Republican White House, it has only exacerbated the problem, and made reform that much more difficult.

What is the BBG's track record? It must be acknowledged at the outset that no other sector of American public diplomacy in recent years has shown the vision and drive of the broadcasting sector under the Broadcasting Board of Governors. The BBG under the leadership of Norman Pattiz, a broadcasting executive and billionaire with extraordinary entrepreneurial ability, has attempted to infuse the staid world of government broadcasting with the competitive spirit of commercial radio in the United States in an effort to meet more effectively the challenges posed to us by the current state of public opinion in the Muslim world.[5] In the process, the BBG has launched several major initiatives over the last several years targeted at Middle Eastern audiences—Radio Sawa, an Arabic-language popular music radio station geared to young people throughout the Arab world, Radio Farda, a similar station directed at Iran, and Al Hurra, an Arabic-language satellite television station. Though it is too early to gauge the ultimate success of these ventures in attracting and influencing audiences in the region, polling data show that they have done surprisingly well, particularly Radio Sawa.[6]

Less visible have been costs and tradeoffs associated with these initiatives. In the process of building Radio Sawa, to begin with, the BBG eliminated the old Arabic service of the Voice of America, and it has made extensive cuts in other language services as well, including the popular Worldwide English (reduced from 24 to 19 hours per day).[7] It is true that VOA Arabic never commanded more than an anemic 1–2% audience share in the region, but this was largely an influential elite audience of government officials and professionals, and much of the reason for it was poor signal quality given the low priority accorded to Arabic-language broadcasting during the Cold War. In spite of assurances that Radio Sawa, once having built a following, would expand beyond popular music and rudimentary news into more serious programming, it seems clear that the BBG never had a clear strategy for doing this, and in fact is reluctant to do so now for fear it will endanger the audience base the radio now enjoys.[8] In the case of Radio Farda, the entire concept seems flawed owing to the fact that the Iranian airwaves were already virtually saturated with Western popular music (although Farda has more extensive news and features than Sawa). But Al Hurra is the most questionable of these ventures, given both its huge expense (some $62 m in start-up costs and an annual operating budget of $37 m), the stiff competition for the television audience in the Arab world today, and the skepticism that pervades the region concerning official U.S. broadcasting and, indeed, all government broadcasting. Strikingly, Congress has never held hearings to consider these stations, nor has it ever formally authorized them.

All of this has led recently to a virtually open revolt against the BBG within the ranks at the Voice of America. Nearly half of the thousand VOA employees signed a petition in July 2004 protesting the "piece-by-piece dismantling" of the Voice and the diversion of funds from it to new programs that are not subject to the same journalistic standards and monitoring as VOA's.[9] That the BBG is pursuing a conscious strategy aimed at the eventual demise of VOA is perhaps an exaggeration, but it does seem to be the case that the Board cares little for the historic roles and missions either of the Voice or of the surrogate radios. In fact, what it seems to be doing is deliberately eroding the differences between VOA and the surrogate radios. Radio Farda is the most instructive case in point. Farda represents an unprecedented amalgam of VOA and the Farsi service of Radio Liberty (it is formally owned by RFE-RL, but has VOA staff detailed to it), broadcasting twenty-four hours a day on three shifts, two out of Prague (the RL headquarters) and one out of Washington. The station is thus more attuned and responsive to audience interests and needs than VOA typically was in the past, yet it makes little effort to present itself as anything other than an American broadcasting operation. This may or may not be a good thing; what is clear is that it is a radical departure from the past, and a course the BBG has embarked on with little awareness on the part of our nation's elected officials.

It would be one thing if the BBG had developed a strategy to match its "vision" and a management structure or process to implement its strategy. Unfortunately, this is far from the case. According to multiple authoritative reports, the BBG is a highly dysfunctional organization. It is a part-time committee (it meets once a month or so) that is attempting to act as the chief executive officer of a large corporation. Moreover, this is a corporation that is more like a holding company made up of a variety of highly independent and yet also sometimes directly competing firms. With no one individual really in charge, members have become accustomed to freelancing according to their own particular interests, setting up personal fiefs, and meddling in personnel and other operational issues, while not providing coherent overall direction or discipline to the enterprise as a whole. Meanwhile, State Department interest and involvement has dwindled to the vanishing point. The result is the astonishing anomaly of a federal agency (the International Broadcasting Bureau) being managed—or mismanaged—by a collection of private citizens that is subject to no effective oversight or control by the executive branch.[10]

As for the Congress, while there is indeed some unhappiness with this situation,[11] the weight of what has become habit, the lack of incentives on the part of members to engage themselves in an obscure foreign policy controversy, and their own effective lobbying efforts have so far protected the BBG from frontal challenge. A key factor, however, has been the role played in all this by Senator Joseph Biden (D-Del.), currently minority leader of the Senate Foreign Relations Committee. Biden has consistently given political cover to Norman Pattiz and otherwise empowered the Board's Democratic members, who from the beginning have pursued an agenda of removing U.S. international broadcasting from the effective control of the government. This connection became public in mid-2005, when President Bush refused to reappoint Pattiz to the BBG (apparently because he was signatory to an advertisement in the *New York Times* in the fall of 2004 opposing Bush's reelection), but later yielded after Biden put a hold on the appointment of Dina Powell as Karen Hughes' deputy at the State Department.[12]

Apart from these political eddies, the nub of the problem is that the BBG as currently constituted is dominated by a parochial broadcasting perspective, and has at best an uncertain grasp of the global context of American public diplomacy or the substantive objectives that public diplomacy should pursue. Accordingly, it has been unable to devise or articulate an overall international broadcasting strategy in anything but the crudest terms. Like the State Department's ill-starred Charlotte Beers, the BBG has not been able to get beyond the thought that the key objective of American public diplomacy is simply to advertise the good things of American life and so make us more liked and appreciated. It does not see the need to articulate the meaning of America in any sophisticated way, to make arguments in defense of American foreign policy, or to shape foreign cultures over the longer term.

Moreover, and this is a key point, to the extent that the BBG does have a strategy, that strategy focuses in a highly parochial manner on the war on terror, and especially on the Middle East. The BBG has thrown money at Middle East public diplomacy while at the same time neglecting and starving the traditional instruments of public diplomacy directed to the rest of the world. It has closed down VOA language services such as Portuguese to Brazil, ostensibly on budget grounds, but actually on the basis of a tacit policy assumption that Latin America weighs little in the scale of American priorities in the war on terror compared to the Middle East. Yet this is in fact by no means clear. Muslims and Islamic terrorist organizations have a presence in Latin America too; the operational impact of American public diplomacy there may be proportionally much greater than what can be achieved in the Middle East; and in any case the United States has important stakes in the future evolution of Brazil. But such strategic reasoning seems completely absent in the BBG's decisions on these matters.

What should be done? First of all, let it be said again that there is much to admire in what the BBG has accomplished, and our new Middle East broadcasting capabilities hold promise in spite of whatever flawed conceptions may be embedded in them. It is therefore by no means clear that Radio Sawa or Radio Farda should be simply abandoned. What is clear, however, is that they need to be subjected to a zero-based review by an external panel of some sort made up of broadcasting and policy experts and entirely independent of the BBG. A similar review should be undertaken of Al Hurra, where the burden of proof remains very much with those supporting this experiment, given its enormous opportunity costs relative to other public diplomacy instruments. What is urgently needed, however, is an overall approach which appreciates and tries to advance our more traditional public diplomacy in the Middle East or the Muslim world generally, with its focus on elites rather than the young or "the street." In particular, it would be a profound mistake to allow further deterioration in the Voice of America generally, or the fragmentation of its capabilities into a series of new and increasingly privatized and commercial-style regional broadcasting entities such as now exists for the Middle East.

Having said this, it is important to appreciate the frustrations the BBG has experienced in its dealings with the Voice of America. The BBG (like USIA before it) has faced in VOA an organizational culture that is highly resistant to change and hampered by what can only be called a trade union mentality (and not accidentally, as noted earlier, VOA has the second oldest work force in the Federal government). Civil service regulations tend to discourage personnel turnover, innovation, and creativity. And as we have seen, the ideological culture of the Voice resists any attempt by management to shape programming so as to be responsive to national needs and the evolving external environment as distinct from the perceived imperatives of American journalism. Accordingly, the BBG has been careful to establish its new radio and television organizations outside of and on a separate basis from the Voice. Radio Sawa and Al Hurra resemble the surrogate radios rather than VOA in that they are private corporations receiving BBG grants; their employees do not have civil service status, and are much easier to hire and fire than VOA employees.

Two questions emerge from this discussion. The first has to do with the relationship between VOA and the surrogate radios that was raised a moment ago. The second has to do with the future status of VOA itself. Specifically, is there an argument after all for privatizing the Voice of America?

There seems to be a growing sentiment within the international broadcasting world that it is time to reconsider the traditional distinction between government and surrogate broadcasting.[13] That there has been a significant erosion in this distinction since the end of the Cold War is clear. While it is true that the countries targeted by Radio Free Asia and Radio Marti remain communist or authoritarian, RFE-RL has had to accommodate itself to vast political changes in Eastern Europe and the former Soviet Union, above all the creation of at least nominally democratic governments and local media enjoying at least a substantial amount of freedom of speech. In some cases, now including most of Eastern Europe, the rationale for maintaining these services in any form has weakened to such an extent that they were seen to lose their basic utility and legitimacy (and did lose much of their audience); they have since been shut down or transitioned to some form of local control. In the services remaining (such as the Russian), their mission has been more or less openly redefined as serving as a kind of check on governmental interference with the local media and providing niche coverage of certain controversial issues that tend to be avoided by them (such as Russian military involvement in Chechnya). At the same time, the Voice has tended to give more focused coverage of news in the countries it broadcasts to, including the use of reporters on the ground and features geared to local interests. In places like Africa, where local media are undeveloped and frequently manipulated by governments, VOA has tended to assume a de facto surrogate role.

Originally, the distinction between government and surrogate broadcasting was widely understood to mean that the surrogate radios were kept at a distance by government in order to permit them to be more aggressive or "propagandistic" than was appropriate for a government broadcaster. As noted earlier, however, the "propagandistic" orientation of the original RFE and RL organizations had essentially been discarded by the beginning of the 1960s. Today, there is virtually no difference between the way the Voice of America and the surrogate radios understand their mission in terms of professionalism of tone or balance and objectivity in news coverage. There may well be some vestigial benefit in maintaining formal "deniability" of U.S. government responsibility for the content or policies of the surrogate radios, but it is surely not more than that, given the virtually universal understanding nowadays that these stations are wholly owned and operated by the U.S. government.

There are a number of strong arguments for consolidating the surrogate radios and the Voice in a single U.S. overseas broadcasting agency. Currently, the BBG controls ninety-seven language services, with a 55% overlap between VOA and the surrogates. Merging the overlapping services would not only bring significant economies but also eliminate both programmatic redundancy (separate news operations above all) and the potential for conflicting messages. Personnel systems and support services would be harmonized, and the management burden of running these complex and diverse operations generally eased. But perhaps the most important benefit is that it would afford the flexibility to ratchet up or down the intensity or type of programming to particular countries according to the situation there, without raising the awkward political and diplomatic issues that necessarily arise in any decision to create (or abolish) new surrogate services. This flexibility might even extend to the creation of broadcasting services with separate identities, such as Radio Sawa or Radio Farda.[14]

This begs, of course, the thorny question of the basis on which such a merger would occur. It has generally been taken for granted that any consolidation of the radios would come at the expense of the surrogates—that is, that the surrogates would effectively be abolished, cannibalized, or folded into the Voice of America.[15] But this is not necessarily the only solution. The Voice, as indicated earlier, leaves something to be desired as a model for overseas broadcasting in today's world. Many of its problems are caused or exacerbated by its status as a federal agency under civil service regulations, which discourages personnel turnover and fosters a trade union outlook that is at odds with journalistic creativity and innovation. The question accordingly arises as to whether it would not make more sense to move in the direction of defederalizing VOA—that is, to assimilate VOA to the status of the surrogate radios, not the other way around.

RFE-RL has been far from immune to the sorts of problems that trouble the Voice, particularly when it was headquartered in Munich and subject as a result to highly inflexible German labor laws. Today, however, managers of the surrogate stations have a great deal of leeway in personnel matters, and that should not be lightly surrendered. As discussed earlier in the context of a revived USIA, it would seem highly desirable to have a personnel system throughout the U.S. overseas broadcasting organizations that would accommodate short tours by mid-career professionals from the private sector, retirees with unique backgrounds and skill sets, and the like. The key requirement is a work force that is well-educated, linguistically able, sophisticated with respect to international events and the policies and interests of the United States, and—to say it again—creative.

Defederalization of the Voice of America, fulfilling as it appears to the logic if not the actual position of the Stanton Commission, begs the obvious question of control. Yet there is an important distinction between defederalizing and privatizing. A defederalized broadcasting entity could well exist within a system of oversight firmly anchored in the policy agencies of the government; indeed, at least in principle, such a system might actually feature stronger control mechanisms than we have had for VOA in the past. As is the case with a variety of other quasi-governmental organizations such as the party-affiliated institutes supported by the National Endowment for Democracy or Federally Funded Research and Development Centers (FFRDCs), control of such a broadcasting entity could be maintained in indirect ways by careful conditioning of granted funds, close monitoring of performance, and management of personnel.

A solution with the following main features would seem to make sense, both in itself and as a political matter. First, I would argue, the Voice of America should be "defederalized" and merged with the surrogate radios to form a single broadcasting entity. Second, the legislative charter of the Broadcasting Board of Governors should be rewritten (and its name changed) to make clear that it is a purely advisory organization with no operational authority over any U.S. broadcasting entity.[16] Third, the International Broadcasting Bureau should be made an integral part of a new United States Information Agency.

The fundamental thrust of such a reform would be to reassert in unambiguous fashion the principle of U.S. government control of the international broadcasting entities it currently funds. At the same time, however, it would also accept the necessity—a necessity grounded in functional as well as political requirements—of maintaining a certain distance between the U.S. government and its overseas broadcasting operations. This distance may be seen, first, in the subordination of the IBB not to the department or secretary of state but to a revived USIA, a move designed to minimize interference in broadcasting operations for tactical diplomatic reasons as distinct from reasons of strategic public diplomacy—an absolute requirement for an effective broadcasting entity. It may be seen, second, in the defederalized status of the broadcasting organizations themselves, which creates a further buffer against direct or directive interference in day-to-day broadcasting decisions by policy officials.[17]

Reconciling policy control with day-to-day autonomy in this way may seem to some like squaring a circle, but I believe the actual history of these organizations shows that such concerns are much exaggerated. Even in the days of CIA sponsorship of RFE and RL, control of the radios by the agency was more theoretical than real. Moreover, there may well be formal mechanisms that could be put in place to ensure that the modalities of policy intervention in broadcasting operations are well understood and appropriately constrained. Such mechanisms might include, for example, a formal channel that would permit the State Department to raise concerns about the coverage of diplomatically sensitive issues with policy officials at USIA/IBB and establish a procedure for adjudicating such concerns. Or they might include a set of crisis response procedures that would temporarily relax the barriers and shorten the distance between policymakers and operators in the broadcasting organizations under certain defined circumstances. (This latter subject will be discussed further below.)

All of this implies, however, that the idea of maintaining a somehow impermeable "firewall" between policy and broadcasting operations, to use the term favored by the current BBG and by liberals in Congress, is fundamentally unworkable and indeed nonsensical. There simply has to be some strategic direction and ultimate accountability for broadcasting entities wholly funded by the American taxpayer; the current situation is little short of scandalous. In any event, the new rules of the road that any such system would require would need to be spelled out in the form of a new (and perhaps legislatively blessed) doctrinal statement. Such a statement, while building on the VOA Charter, would extend and qualify it in ways that would give it real clarity and operational utility. While undoubtedly controversial, such a step would be much more politically saleable, it may be argued, in the context of a defederalized VOA and the relative autonomy such status would necessarily confer.

CHAPTER 9

The Defense Department: Into the Act?

As indicated earlier, the term "strategic communication" has gained traction within the defense establishment over the last year or so as a useful (and usefully bland) generic term covering psychological operations, the military equivalent of public diplomacy, and defense public affairs. Yet the term itself, and the relationship between these three disciplines, remains highly problematic.[1] Existing PSYOP forces are geared primarily to tactical- or operational-level support of U.S. troops in combat; whether or to what extent PSYOP has or should have a "strategic" component is unclear and controversial. To further confuse the situation, PSYOP has recently been grouped with several other capabilities that are highly technical in nature—electronic warfare, computer network operations, operational security, and deception—to form the new discipline of "information operations" (IO).[2] Defense public affairs is oriented to the servicing of the domestic American media, and is accordingly sensitive to any suggestion that there is an ulterior ("strategic") motive in its approach to managing the media. The military-media relationship has been politically neuralgic ever since the Vietnam War, and the weight of such sensitivities within the Pentagon cannot be overestimated, to say nothing of the Congress. Finally, it should be noted that the term "public diplomacy" has no real standing in current military doctrine, nor any entity in the defense establishment clearly identified with it. Typically, strategic communication is now generally said to include "(defense) support for public diplomacy" rather than public diplomacy proper, which is considered a State rather than Defense Department responsibility; an illustration of this role is the use of DoD assets (such as the Commando Solo aircraft) to rebroadcast Voice of America programming. Nevertheless, the Office of the Secretary of Defense (OSD, the civilian side of the Pentagon) has periodically felt a need to create some organizational capability for public diplomacy in a more robust sense. As discussed earlier, this has included the declassification and publication of intelligence information (for example, in the *Soviet Military Power* series produced annually by the Pentagon in the 1980s) and counterpropaganda or counterdisinformation activities.[3]

Part of the problem here lies in continuing uncertainty concerning the nature and scope of psychological operations among practitioners in the field as well as outsiders. Current doctrine tends to describe PSYOP in very expansive and vague language, as in the following official DoD definition: "Planned operations to convey selected information and indicators to foreign audiences to influence their emotions, motives, objective reasoning, and ultimately the behavior of foreign governments, organizations, groups, and individuals."[4] Oddly, nothing in this definition actually distinguishes PSYOP from public diplomacy as practiced by civilian agencies of the U.S. government, let alone from other information-related activities of U.S. military forces or the Department of Defense. If PSYOP at least at the "strategic" level is virtually indistinguishable from public diplomacy, however, it becomes difficult to see why the Defense Department should play an independent role in it. It also imposes requirements for coordination with broader policy that have always proven difficult to handle as a bureaucratic matter. This is partly because PSYOP is not well understood at higher reaches of the defense establishment or the national security bureaucracy more generally, but partly also because of the unsavory connotations the term continues to have for many, including many within the defense establishment itself.[5] Even within the special operations community, which has organizational "ownership" of PSYOP (the U.S. Army Civil Affairs and Psychological Operations Command is a component of the joint U.S. Special Operations Command), PSYOP is not always well understood and has never been considered a high priority by its senior leadership.[6]

There is now a general recognition within the Pentagon that this situation needs to change if DoD and the U.S. government as a whole are to engage effectively in strategic communication. Opinion is sharply divided, however, on how to proceed. Some believe that the solution lies in greatly enhanced coordination between PSYOP, public diplomacy, and public affairs within DoD, at the interagency or national level, and in the field. Others feel such an approach is fundamentally unrealistic, and argue that the most immediate need is rather to sort out the "lanes in the road" that separate or should separate these various disciplines. While not denying the need for enhanced coordination, they argue rather that the only way to attain it is precisely through a clearer delineation of their respective roles and missions.[7]

There are several distinct issues here. One is the proper relationship between PSYOP and public diplomacy; the other is whether it is realistic to consider public affairs a tool of "strategic communications" at all.

The military PSYOP community has been sensitized over the years to the deep unpopularity of PSYOP in the wider culture, and for this reason has come to have an institutional stake in describing the PSYOP mission in the most benign possible terms. Moreover, many PSYOPers have come to embrace for reasons of their own what one may call an idealistic view of their mission. They tend to stress its humanitarian impact, arguing that it saves enemy as well as friendly lives (often but not always true); and they insist that PSYOP only deals in "truth," which has the effect of assimilating it still further to public diplomacy or public affairs. This "hearts and flowers" tendency in the PSYOP world, as it is characterized by critics, is a reality that should not be underestimated.[8] The military PSYOP community has also consistently pushed for greater and more responsive policy guidance to PSYOP practitioners from senior levels of DoD and the national security bureaucracy generally, and closer coordination between PSYOP and other instruments of strategic communications. Just as consistently, these efforts have been rebuffed, and senior military and civilian officials alike have continued to distrust the PSYOP instrument and to keep their distance from it.[9] This has contributed to a perennial problem in securing approval of PSYOP themes and products from policy officials in a timely fashion—which in turn reinforces the skepticism in various quarters concerning the fundamental utility of PSYOP.

As might be expected, American PSYOP capabilities have been utilized extensively in the ongoing conflicts in Afghanistan and Iraq. Indeed, the American invasion of Iraq and the run-up to it saw the most massive PSYOP campaign by the U.S. military since Vietnam. This included, among other things, intensive efforts using email and other channels to persuade Iraqi military commanders not to use the weapons of mass destruction they were presumed to control and heavy leafleting of deployed Iraqi forces, beginning well before the actual outbreak of hostilities. Press accounts provide a partial window into the activities and achievements of U.S. PSYOP forces there.[10] While much still remains opaque in the public record, numerous "lessons learned" studies undertaken within the U.S. military have permitted at least a preliminary assessment of the overall performance of these forces and identified directions for the future. Recently, a study conducted by Christopher Lamb under the auspices of the National Defense University has comprehensively reviewed these internal documents and provided a wide range of recommended changes.[11]

According to the Lamb study, American combat commanders in recent conflicts voiced frequent complaints about the lack of responsiveness and general effectiveness of PSYOP units in direct support of military operations. Apart from shortfalls in funding, equipment, and trained personnel that are chronic in the PSYOP forces, it holds that the underlying problem here is a tension or disconnect between PSYOP at the tactical and at the theater level, and more fundamentally, between the tactical mission of support for combat commanders and the theater mission of providing generic information in support of American strategic and political goals. It argues that there has been an imbalance in PSYOP activities in favor of the theater mission, in spite of the fact that it is at the tactical level that PSYOP provides the greatest value added, and suggests that the theater-level PSYOP organization (the Joint Psychological Operations Task Force) should concentrate on supporting the operating PSYOP forces rather than in theater-level information dissemination. This latter mission, it further suggests, might be better performed by a separate "public diplomacy" operation of some kind. The comparative advantage of PSYOP as a military instrument is clearly on or near the battlefield, in close conjunction with and support of actual operations or their aftermath; and it differs critically from public diplomacy in that it can leverage the psychological impact of military operations to effect immediate change in the behavior of target audiences, not simply to influence attitudes over time. To cite a key recent DoD document, the primary mission of PSYOP is best described as "aggressive behavior modification of adversaries at the operational and tactical level of war"; support for public diplomacy may be a secondary or collateral mission.[12]

The Lamb study identifies four broad mission areas for PSYOP: "isolating an adversary from domestic and international support," "reducing the effectiveness of an adversary's forces," "deterring escalation by adversarial leadership," and "minimizing collateral damage." Only the first of these has significant overlap with public diplomacy as traditionally understood. The study also emphasizes the need to move away from the simplistic conceptualization of PSYOP as "truthful" toward a more operationally useful notion of persuasion as a combination of appeals to reason and to emotion. As it tellingly notes:

The observation that one must manipulate emotion effectively would not surprise marketing specialists, but it would be considered more suspect in U.S. Government persuasive communication disciplines such as public diplomacy and public affairs that deal with the domestic public and friendly or neutral foreign audiences. They would insist that with such audiences, truth and appeals to reason are both more effective and more legitimate. The assertion here is that such is not necessarily the case for PSYOP, which helps to partly explain the unease that exists and unsettles cooperation between these government information activity sets.[13]

PSYOP assets are legitimately used in support of generic public diplomacy in circumstances where those assets offer unique advantages in disseminating public diplomacy materials. There is a long history, for example, of the use of Commando Solo, the PSYOP radio and television broadcasting aircraft operated by the Pennsylvania Air National Guard, for relaying Voice of America broadcasts into a theater of military operations to which the United States has little other easy access. But there is every reason to embrace the refocusing of PSYOP advocated by the Lamb study (though by no means universally accepted in the PSYOP community). At the same time, this does not entirely resolve the issue we have been addressing. The problem is that there has been very inadequate attention to the question whether there is a distinct kind of *public diplomacy* that is properly the responsibility, or the primary responsibility, of the Department of Defense.[14] In the past, as just indicated, DoD (or more precisely, OSD) has from time to time gotten into the public diplomacy business, as in the OSI episode; but it has done so more to fill a vacuum and because of its readier access to funding than because of any carefully elaborated rationale.

In fact, a good case can be made for recognizing a distinct discipline of "defense public diplomacy."[15] During the 1980s, a small office within the Office of the Deputy under secretary for Policy (then General Richard Stilwell) carried out a range of military-related public diplomacy activities on behalf of DoD and the Reagan administration, perhaps most notably, an annual publication entitled *Soviet Military Power,* which broke new ground in making public much previously classified information about a wide range of Soviet military programs and developed a reputation for authoritativeness and a wide readership overseas. The office also sponsored conferences abroad and organized briefings of foreign officials and journalists on controversial security issues of the day. In the current international environment, it is not difficult to imagine a wide range of military-related issues that could profitably be handled by a dedicated public diplomacy staff within the Pentagon, from law of armed combat issues[16] to rules of engagement in Iraq to the global WMD threat to the changing military posture of the United States throughout the world. A particular focus of any such effort would certainly be countering foreign propaganda and disinformation relating to the U.S. military—properly speaking a public diplomacy function rather than a PSYOP function, as often claimed by the PSYOP community.

Implicit in the idea of a distinct discipline of "defense public diplomacy" is the assumption that the kinds of activities it would undertake go well beyond the public affairs function and cannot reasonably be expected to be carried out by public affairs personnel. As discussed earlier, it is the nature of the public affairs function to be reactive rather than proactive and concerned primarily with day-to-day handling of the domestic press. What we are speaking of here is a proactive, strategic effort to shape the international information environment, and to do so over time by means of extended campaigns and not single "fire and forget" actions.

This leads back then to the second question raised earlier, whether the public affairs function can and should be fused with PSYOP and public diplomacy under the single rubric of "strategic communication." There is no easy answer to this, as it can hardly be denied that the boundaries between domestic and foreign audiences and information are increasingly artificial given the technologies of today, and therefore that policymakers cannot afford (if they ever could) to ignore the strategic implications of what their public affairs officers do. While no one can deny the need for reasonably close coordination in these matters, the case seems strong nevertheless that the cultural divide is simply too great to be bridged in this way. I believe that the three functions must remain doctrinally and organizationally distinct if they are to have perceived legitimacy and to function effectively—and if anything, should become more distinct.

The solution I would propose to this dilemma is simple if seemingly radical. In the first place, public affairs should be formally excluded from the "strategic communication" rubric. Second, psychological operations should be redefined and reorganized to focus on its tactical mission, and in the process also be separated formally from "strategic communication." Its disputed strategic—and theater—missions would then be absorbed by defense public diplomacy, which would therefore become coextensive with "strategic communication" as such. This would include in particular the theater broadcasting mission and the assets specifically supporting it. I recognize that PSYOP traditionalists can be expected to resist what they will no doubt see as a major raid on their bureaucratic turf. Doing so, however, would be short-sighted. The time has come to accept the fact that, given the cultural sensitivities involved, PSYOP as currently constituted has crippling liabilities that will continue to stand in the way of its performing a national mission. Refocusing PSYOP in the manner suggested here will in fact, I think, greatly strengthen its perceived legitimacy both within and outside the military and facilitate efforts now underway to modernize it and better integrate it with the combat arms.

The problem then becomes how to approach creating a discipline of defense public diplomacy within the Department of Defense where at present one scarcely exists. This problem cannot be solved merely by cycling PSYOP or public affairs personnel through "strategic communication" slots or offices—though that practice should not be totally excluded through an overly purist interpretation of keeping to one's own "lane in the road." It can only be solved by creating a new cadre of public diplomatists or communicators within the defense establishment, including within the uniformed military itself. "Strategic Communication," like PSYOP itself, should become a military specialty, and career tracks in it created throughout the services.[17] But there is also a need for a substantial, broadly educated civilian cadre that would include regional experts, linguists, intelligence analysts, former journalists and media experts, and academic social scientists (anthropologists and psychologists, notably). Assuming certain kinds of broadcasting operations would belong to the strategic communication function, as makes eminent sense, this cadre would also need to include technical specialists in radio and television as well as in computers and the internet.

The next step would be to create a new institutional infrastructure for strategic communication. Within the uniformed military, a "Joint Strategic Communication Command" could be created to administratively manage the new discipline and provide reach-back support for strategic communications elements deployed in overseas theaters.[18] Such a command should not be subordinate to the U.S. Special Operations Command or to the U.S. Strategic Command (as proponent of Information Operations). A good alternative would be the U.S. Joint Forces Command (JFCOM), given its mission to manage "transformation" in the armed forces to meet current security challenges.[19] It should also be noted that JFCOM is to be the home of a new joint field organization for defense public affairs, the Joint Public Affairs Support Element. Close coordination with this unit would clearly be highly desirable.[20]

In addition, it would be essential to establish a research and training center that does not presently exist—let us call it the "Defense Strategic Communication Institute," ideally to be located in the Washington area. This institute would house regional and functional experts in the fields just mentioned, and would have extensive contractor support. One of its critical functions would be to develop the doctrinal underpinnings of the new strategic communication field. It might also be given training responsibilities that would extend beyond DoD to other government agencies involved in public diplomacy, notably the State Department and (a revived) USIA.[21] Especially given our current wartime strategic environment, a single focal point for public diplomacy training across all agencies would bring immeasurable benefits.

Finally, policy direction for strategic communication would be provided by an "Office of Strategic Communication" under the under secretary of defense for policy. This staff entity would be responsible for coordination with the DoD public affairs office as well as with other public diplomacy organizations and interagency public diplomacy groups. While such an arrangement would not guarantee an end to friction between public affairs and PSYOP/public diplomacy within DoD, it would clarify and simplify responsibilities and reporting relationships.[22] Above all, strategic communication would be visibly severed from the PSYOP/special operations world and brought into close proximity to national policy.[23]

Let us in conclusion address several issues that have been generally ignored in recent discussions of strategic communication. The first concerns tasking authority and support for strategic communication (as we are now calling defense public diplomacy) relative to other parts of the defense bureaucracy. I have mentioned the potential role of strategic communication in preparing and using declassified intelligence information in publications such as *Soviet Military Power*. Why not go further and enable strategic communication personnel to task defense intelligence organizations to collect intelligence against targets of primary interest to them? These might involve, for example, evidence of enemy atrocities, corruption, environmental devastation, and the like. Moreover, the Defense Department invests very substantial resources in photographing and filming military operations and other activities, primarily for historical reasons and secondarily for various public relations uses. There is no reason why combat photographers could not be tasked to photograph or film things of particular interest from a strategic communication point of view; but this has always been resisted by DoD Public Affairs. One possibility that should also be considered in this context is creating dedicated, rapidly deployable field units under the Joint Strategic Communication Command that would search out and record material of interest and transmit the product electronically for use by U.S. broadcasting stations or independent media. This could be a powerful tool in countering disinformation directed against the U.S. armed forces, and also in telling positive stories about developments in remote areas to which the commercial media do not have ready access (or in which they otherwise lack interest).

A second issue has to do with the more conscious and effective utilization of a range of traditional military activities that can be understood as "soft power" resources but are rarely considered in this context.[24] Military officers, first of all, are de facto diplomats, with many opportunities to interact with military counterparts and other government officials from countries all over the world. Friendships formed with foreign officers at relatively early stages in a career can sometimes acquire strategic significance later on, serving as reliable channels for the discreet projection of American influence at high reaches of a foreign government. Defense attachés in American embassies abroad should be treated as diplomatic as much as, if not indeed more than, intelligence resources.[25] The Foreign Area Officer (FAO) program of the Army, and to a lesser degree the other services also, provides a unique capability that should be viewed in this light, and for this and other reasons deserves to be strengthened and expanded. Finally, there is the large and increasingly important area of education and training. The venerable International Military Education and Training (IMET) program is a paradigm of what might be called military political action, but interactions with foreign militaries in a great variety of routine training and exercise activities are a common feature of

American military life today that can undoubtedly be exploited more deliberately than has been the case in the past. Higher military education is another all-important arena. Hundreds of the very best officers of virtually every country in the world regularly attend the four American war colleges each year, and many go on to become heads of their respective services later in their careers. Recently, as part of its overall strategy for "countering ideological support for terrorism," the Department of Defense has revamped and expanded programs for the education of foreign military officers in special regionally oriented centers in Germany, Hawaii, and Washington, D.C.

CHAPTER 10

The White House: Key to the Game?

As was noted at the outset, given the low level of institutionalization of the public diplomacy function within the bureaucracy, it is bound to have difficulty sustaining itself in the absence of high-level political attention. To the extent that this situation is corrected by the kinds of measures proposed here, and in particular by the reconstitution of USIA, a case could be made that it is less essential to involve the president or the White House staff directly in public diplomacy than now seems to be widely accepted as necessary. At the same time, there are legitimate grounds for skepticism as to how appropriate or effective direct White House involvement in this area actually is. The White House as a whole, and particularly staff who pay attention to the press and public opinion, notoriously focus on the immediate rather than the long-term, on the domestic audience rather than the rest of the world, and on the president's agenda narrowly conceived rather than on the broader interests of the nation. Having said this, it is nonetheless essential to try to understand what contribution the White House can usefully make to supporting and improving the public diplomacy or strategic influence capabilities of the U.S. government.

To speak of "the White House" in this context is to speak primarily of the National Security Council (NSC), its permanent support staff (the NSC Staff, part of the Executive Office of the President and headed by the National Security Adviser), and the interagency system that is at least nominally directed by it.[1] As we have seen, however, the White House proper has also had a significant role at least in recent years in public diplomacy in the form of its Office of Global Communications (OGC); in any case, the White House Communications Director and his extensive press or public affairs operation is necessarily a player in this arena. Most of the recent studies of the current condition of American public diplomacy have urged a strengthened role for the National Security Council and its staff, but detailed suggestions vary. Some merely call for more centralized coordination of interagency public diplomacy activities, while begging the question of how this is to be enforced from above.[2] Others have argued for the creation of a new, powerful White House official of some sort to provide greater coherence and direction to the overall public diplomacy effort. The Council on Foreign Relations Report has staked out the most radical position, arguing for a new White House coordinating structure and interagency staff headed by a special public diplomacy adviser to the president, analogous to the National Security Adviser himself, with wide-ranging responsibilities and possibly with operational (command) authority over the bureaucracy. The Defense Science Board has recommended a more realistic solution on similar lines: a new "Deputy National Security Adviser for Strategic Communication" would be created, chairing an under secretary-level interagency Strategic Communication Committee that would "have authority to assign responsibilities and plan the work of departments and agencies . . . concur in strategic communication personnel choices; [and] shape strategic communication budget priorities."[3]

Let us call these suggestions the "Czar" model. A less ambitious version of this approach would create a new Special Counsel to the President for Public Diplomacy with cabinet rank, but with a relatively small office and limited line responsibilities; its chief function would be to establish strategic goals and messages, oversee implementation, and ensure effective measurement of results.[4] This may be called the "Counselor" model. Somewhere between these is a third option, modeled perhaps on the office of the United States Trade Representative. The latter is a cabinet-level position located within the White House (that is, within the Executive Office of the President) but established by legislation and supported by a substantial interagency staff of highly qualified professionals. This "USTR" model would avoid over-centralized control of the interagency process, but instead aim to "leverage" related activities pursued by different agencies and maximize resource synergies.[5]

The problem with White House "czars" and "counselors" has always been that their institutional base is shaky and their exact mandate and authority unclear, while it is rarely easy for them to gain and maintain the ear of the president given the claim to priority of the line agencies in seeking decisions from him.[6] The "Czar" model as sketched above is problematic for another reason, namely, that in seeking to overcome these difficulties it goes to the opposite extreme. The Council on Foreign Relations variant essentially creates a parallel NSC apparatus, posing thereby a severe institutional challenge to the overall authority of the National Security Adviser in the interagency policy process; the dualistic interagency structure it would create is fundamentally unworkable. The Defense Science Board variant is more defensible because it is anchored in the NSC staff itself, but it encounters the same difficulty in that it would create an unworkable rivalry between the new public diplomacy deputy and the principal NSC deputy. But beyond this, there is little chance that a public diplomacy czar would be granted operational authority over public diplomacy activities, implying the power to override decisions made by particular line agencies—particularly when such authority is not exercised otherwise by the NSC or any interagency body, which historically it has never been.

Left vague in most of these organizational prescriptions is just what sort of "public diplomacy" is being talked about. As I argued earlier, the articulation and advocacy of policy is a public diplomacy function that needs to be coupled as closely as possible with the development and implementation of policy as such. But this is much less the case with its educational and cultural functions, or more generally with the entire programmatic side of public diplomacy. From this vantage point, I believe the "USTR" model of White House-centered public diplomacy makes the most sense, with its emphasis on coordination of public diplomacy programs and resources across agencies. The main problem with this alternative, however, is that in spite of its cabinet-level head and its legislative mandate, the new agency is still not likely to have the institutional weight necessary to provide real strategic direction to public diplomacy or to resolve authoritatively interagency disputes over programs and resources. These disputes would probably migrate into regular interagency policy channels, while strategic leadership in this area would remain fragmented.

However, there is a variant of this idea that avoids these difficulties. It is to give the director of the United States Information Agency a "dual-hatted" role as director of a similar White House agency or office.[7] Let us call this the "DCI" model. Until recently, the Director of Central Intelligence was dual-hatted as both Director of the Central Intelligence Agency and DCI, a position responsible for providing coordination of programs and resources across the various agencies making up the so-called "Intelligence Community," and supported by a small staff (the Intelligence Community Staff) independent of the CIA and located near the White House rather than at CIA headquarters in northern Virginia. This arrangement came under much criticism in the debate of the last several years over intelligence reform, on the grounds primarily that the DCI had insufficient authority over the defense components of the Intelligence Community. Under the new intelligence legislation, the DCI would be superseded by a "National Intelligence Director" different from the CIA director who would be given enhanced authority over intelligence budgets and personnel across all agencies. But whatever the merits of the argument for greater centralized control of the Intelligence Community, the situation in the public diplomacy world is quite a different one, and there seems little reason to endow a public diplomacy equivalent of the DCI with this kind of authority over other agencies. Above all, there is no agency in the public diplomacy world comparable in the intelligence world to the Department of Defense, which owns by far the greatest portion of intelligence assets and considers them integral to its mission. Public diplomacy programs of course involve much smaller sums of federal dollars, but they also tend to be on the margins of the activities of most government agencies. There is thus good reason to believe that an adequate level of strategic leadership and coordination could be provided for public diplomacy by a White House-affiliated office[8] headed by the USIA director, the owner of most public diplomacy programs and therefore the natural leader of the "community" of agencies engaged in public diplomacy.

A dual-hatted role for the USIA director would have the very considerable added advantage that it would strengthen the bureaucratic position of an organization that has always been weak relative to the major national security agencies of the U.S. government. Above all, it would provide real institutional grounding for the advisory relationship between the director and the president in this area that in the past has existed only or mostly on paper. But it is important too to appreciate the logic behind it. Public diplomacy and intelligence have something very significant in common: they are strictly speaking policy support functions, not policy functions, but for just this reason they are—or should be—pervasively present in all the policy agencies of the national security bureaucracy. Accordingly, it is useful to have a mechanism that permits each, while having its own—indispensable—institutional home, to reach across and into the policy agencies to nurture their respective functions and coordinate and sustain related operations.

Having said all this, it would be well to insist on an important difference between the roles and missions of a White House-affiliated public diplomacy office and the DCI/IC Staff. In the public diplomacy case, it is essential—or so I shall argue—that the scope of the office be defined more broadly than public diplomacy in the bureaucratic sense we have been discussing. As noted earlier, there is a range of activities carried out by U.S. government agencies that have never or not usually been understood as public diplomacy proper, but are clearly akin to it and directly or indirectly support it. These include most prominently humanitarian activities of all kinds—disaster relief, food assistance, global public health efforts, and the like. These activities fall largely under the purview of the Agency for International Development. But there is also an array of technical assistance, education and training programs (such as the International Military Education and Training program discussed a moment ago) that can be found throughout both the national security and the domestic agencies of the U.S. government. Finally, they also include programs supporting democracy-building and human rights abroad, some of which are carried out currently by the State Department, others by private grantees of the National Endowment for Democracy. Many such programs are linked weakly if at all to any strategic purpose or coordinated in any systematic way with other interested agencies. Looked at in this perspective, the new entity we are contemplating is most properly understood as a kind of bureaucratic focal point for American "soft power" programs and resources generally.

It is important to emphasize, though, that the idea here is not to create another bureaucracy, but rather a small and lean organization that represents in effect a kind of consortium of independent agencies and operates largely on a consensus basis. Its staff would consist primarily of detailees from agencies other than USIA. Like the Intelligence Community Staff, much of its activity would be concentrated in the area of finance and budgets. The organization's name should reflect this broader mandate—perhaps "Office of the Director of

Foreign Information and Assistance." Recognizing the important USAID equities involved here, the legislative charter of the organization might also specify that a senior official of that agency be dual-hatted as the Deputy Director.[9] This would also dovetail nicely with the recent change announced by Secretary of State Rice, as discussed earlier, that would bring the AID director physically into the State Department and give him "dual-hatted" authority over other assistance-type programs within state.

Let us turn briefly to consider the policy information dimension of public diplomacy in the White House. The key point returns to the argument made earlier concerning the State Department: it is essential that policy information be considered an integral part of the policy process, and not an afterthought that can be entrusted to "non-substantive" public diplomacy specialists. If this is so, I believe, it is a mistake to try to create an elaborate public diplomacy structure within the White House or in the National Security Council system (along the lines, for example, of the NSDD 77 committees mentioned earlier, or the scheme proposed in the Council on Foreign Relations Report). Rather, what is needed in the White House is what might be called a cultural adjustment, such that public diplomacy strategies and initiatives are routinely included as a key aspect of policy development within the NSC staff and throughout the interagency system. Such a cultural adjustment would not be easy, but neither is it utopian. A State Department more attuned to the importance of public diplomacy would obviously greatly facilitate any such change, and in fact would make less necessary constant intervention from the NSC staff or elsewhere in the White House to ensure that public diplomacy issues are given their due in the policy process. At the same time, to the extent that it is found necessary to use individuals largely or solely as public diplomacy specialists, they should be firmly embedded within policy shops rather than isolated in their own bureaucratic ghettoes.

Something needs to be said about the question of the extent to which it is possible or desirable under all circumstances to maintain centralized control of policy information. This relates specifically to the role the White House should play here, but it has broader significance as well. Many of the problems with public diplomacy in the State Department have to do with the cumbersome system of internal clearances that are required for approval of even the most routine actions. In the psychological operations realm, the United States has regularly been hampered by the perceived need to gain approval of particular PSYOP products at very high levels of the Department of Defense. A recent internal analysis of DoD PSYOP practice has rightly criticized this tendency and called for a new approach involving a conscious acceptance of risk in balancing the requirements of policy control with the requirements of timeliness and effectiveness.[10] Those defending the alternative approach often point to the poor quality of the personnel carrying out these operations or their inadequate training or both; but the solution only further discourages initiative at the working level and drives away competent and energetic personnel. It is encouraging that Karen Hughes has recently established a new policy allowing ambassadors to respond to breaking news issues without clearance from Washington. The importance for effective public diplomacy of "empowering the field" in this manner cannot be overstated.[11]

Having said this, it should be added that there may be special circumstances under which top-down control of public diplomacy information is desirable and indeed necessary. Such circumstances would certainly include, for example, the immediate aftermath of the 9/11 attacks, or other crisis situations involving the actual or potential use of force by the United States. In the past, little systematic thought seems to have been given to the crisis management dimension of public diplomacy.[12] There are many complexities here that need to be analyzed carefully and prepared for in advance. In crisis situations, for example, the normal distinction between public diplomacy and public affairs becomes blurred, as every statement by government spokesmen is scrutinized at home and abroad for strategic meaning. Accordingly, there is an operational requirement to break down at least to some extent the "lanes in the road" separating these disciplines and to bring together public diplomacy and public affairs personnel in what might be called a crisis information cell within a larger crisis management committee structure. And to come back to a point raised earlier, the pressures of time in a crisis may also impose a requirement for operational decision-making that short-circuits established interagency protocols and procedures. This is a topic I cannot pursue further here, except to note that it has become a very live issue in recent discussions of reform of the National Security Council staff and system to reflect the realities of the contemporary security environment.

Having said all this, a case can certainly be made for retaining a high-level interagency committee relating to public diplomacy under NSC auspices. But I would propose broadening the scope of such a committee beyond that of the existing Policy Coordinating Committee on Strategic Communication, so as to encompass the entire range of "soft power" issues described a moment ago. As such, this PCC would merge with or incorporate the current PCC on "Democracy, Human Rights, and International Operations." It might then be called something like the "Policy Coordinating Committee on Foreign Information, Assistance, and Democracy Promotion." It could be cochaired (as the Strategic Communication PCC was supposed to be) by a senior NSC official and the under secretary of State for Public Diplomacy and Public Affairs,[13] but on the assumption that the under secretary would now be responsible for the democracy and human rights portfolio within the State Department, as discussed earlier. This PCC would then be aligned in terms of its scope both with the State Department's new internal organization and with the White House Office of Foreign Information and Assistance. It would provide the strategic and policy guidance this new entity would require in carrying out its (operational and programmatic) functions.

CHAPTER 11

Strategic Influence and the Future

The focus of this study has been on the U.S. government and how it can more effectively perform the public diplomacy function. Yet this is only part of a larger picture, and it is essential in concluding to say something about that picture. As many observers have noted, all governments today suffer to some extent from a credibility problem in communicating with foreign audiences (and often their own populations). This is especially true in the Middle East, where governments have long exercised significant levels of control over print and broadcast media and discouraged public debate of political issues or public criticism of government policies. And it is especially true for the United States, in the Middle East and elsewhere, given the grip of anti-Americanism today on political elites throughout much of the world. These considerations, as noted earlier, raise serious questions about the wisdom of creating an American satellite television broadcasting capability for the Middle East, as the Broadcasting Board of Governors has proceeded to do with Al-Hurra. Accordingly, it is vital for the United States to explore the potential for a kind of public diplomacy importantly different from public diplomacy in the past, one that relies to a much greater degree on the "indirect approach" (to borrow Liddell Hart's famous characterization of the British way of war)—that is to say, on allies and proxies of various kinds.

To begin with, there is the question of the relationship of U.S. public diplomacy activities to those of allied and friendly governments around the world. This is a subject strikingly neglected in the literature on American public diplomacy as well as in current practice.[1] A useful recent study by a British think tank has emphasized the need for the advanced democracies to take a more multilateral approach to public diplomacy rather than treating it implicitly as a zero-sum competition, part of the traditional "Great Game" of major power diplomacy.[2] At the very least, nominally friendly western governments should not simply be given a pass by the United States if, as happened recently in the case of France, their public diplomacy efforts are reoriented to make common cause with other countries suffering from supposed American cultural dominance.[3] More generally, though, it ought to be possible to engage our allies and other friendly countries on public diplomacy, particularly in the context of the global war on terror, to a much greater degree than we have hitherto. We could explore ways in which, for example, certain countries could develop niche capabilities and missions in this area,[4] crisis coordination with allies could be enhanced, and long-range planning efforts coordinated. Joint initiatives could be undertaken to sponsor and fund a variety of private sector activities, perhaps particularly educational ventures in the Muslim world, or for that matter in Europe.[5]

This brings us to the question of private sector involvement in public diplomacy. There is nothing new in this: governments, and in particular the United States, have long supported private sector activities—educational and cultural exchange programs notably—deemed to have a positive impact on their foreign policies. At present, however, it can be argued that there is real urgency in broadening the reach of public diplomacy not only beyond governments but also beyond the limited sectors or institutions of western societies that have traditionally engaged in it. This might mean in the first instance lessening reliance on elite universities as the locus of exchange programs in favor of universities specializing in more practical or technical subjects such as journalism, computer science, or agricultural economics. But it would also mean looking beyond the academic world to (perhaps above all) the business community, both at home and abroad,[6] to elements of the popular culture, to foreign diasporas, and to non-governmental organizations (NGOs) of all kinds, which have undergone explosive growth in very recent years and have a presence throughout the world which it is difficult for governments to replicate. In all of these cases, the credibility factor is fundamental in making them more attractive public diplomacy vehicles than government spokesmen, even with the inevitable lessening of government control that this entails.

The key challenge here is for the U.S. government to make a case to these various communities that they are a vital weapon in the unconventional war against radical Islamism that we are being forced to wage. In the case of the extensive Arab and Muslim diasporas in the United States, for example, we have here cultural and linguistic resources not otherwise available to the nation that can prove invaluable if properly managed; but managing them will not be an easy task. Unconventional strategies will need to be pursued by the U.S. government as a whole, not just its public diplomacy components, to incentivize, recruit and employ effectively a pool of hyphenated Americans of all kinds for ongoing public diplomacy operations or in a reserve or contingency role for similar purposes. Above all, there needs to be an extensive effort to reach out to Muslim Americans of a moderate religious bent who can engage and criticize the tenets of radical Islamism with credibility and effect.

It is necessary to return for a moment to the question discussed at length earlier of the adverse impact of contemporary American political culture on the conduct of public diplomacy or influence operations. It may well be that nothing can be said or done to alter attitudes or standard operating procedures in the prestige media that do demonstrable damage to American national interests in the war on terror. But at the very least, it is time for the media to engage in some serious introspection regarding their responsibilities to the nation as a whole for sustaining American "soft power" in the largest sense of the term— or for others to call them to account. For example, it is far from evident that media exploitation of the appalling photographs of abusive behavior by American soldiers in Abu Ghraib prison in Baghdad was required by some immutable journalistic standard of probity. It is one thing to report stories of this sort, but quite another to retail the most lurid images of cruelty, death, and destruction in ways guaranteed to spread them around the world and so cause incalculable harm to the U.S. government and to the reputation of America as a society and civilization. But is it too much to ask the media to think twice about the way such stories are reported? The sad truth is that many in the media took satisfaction in embarrassing the military and their own government by these revelations, and took no trouble to present them in a balanced way or in a larger perspective (which would recognize, for example, that many more terrible things are done in war and have in fact been done in this war). When our own media are producing material which at the end of the day is virtually indistinguishable from the propaganda of our enemies, something seems to have gone seriously wrong in our society. It is equally wrong when such material is opportunistically exploited by the political opposition in ways that can only aid and comfort those same enemies.

In fact, however, the U.S. government, and the military in particular, are not without levers to use against the commercial media, and perhaps the time has come for a reconsideration of this subject as well. These levers include such mundane things as access for reporters to senior government officials or to military information otherwise not readily obtainable. It is difficult to fathom why certain reporters for media such as the *New York Times* are regularly granted access to—or are able to arrange leaks from—the most senior levels of the government about the most sensitive imaginable subjects, such as the recent stories concerning supposed secret CIA prisons in Europe. At the end of this road lies the option of legal action against individual reporters or their organizations.

But the media are not alone among elements of American society capable of compromising the effectiveness of American soft power in the current global conflict. Hollywood is another. There is of course a long history of the Hollywood studios working cooperatively with the government and military in times of war, and there is no reason they should not be expected to do so now. Given the predominant political complexion of today's Hollywood, however, it would perhaps be more realistic simply to hope that harm from that quarter can be kept at tolerable levels. It would be helpful, for example, if Hollywood would refrain from portrayals of Islam and Muslims that are inflammatory or disrespectful—or, on the other hand, that appear to validate terrorist arguments or glorify their cause. The wisdom of making any films at all about the Crusades of the Middle Ages might perhaps be questioned, given the very vivid folk memories of this episode still alive in the Arab world.[7] Of course, the highly sexualized content of many Hollywood movies is highly offensive to most Muslims, and provides grist for the propaganda mill of the radical Islamists. On this front, one can only despair.

Finally, though, it would be unfair not to mention a recurring problem at the other end of the political spectrum. Statements by evangelical Christian ministers denigrating Islam as a religion, though no doubt not taken very seriously in this country, have a disproportionate impact in the Muslim world, unaccustomed as it is to the idea of a wall between church and state. Such comments are assumed by many to represent official attitudes, and reinforce the notion that the West (with Israel) is out to destroy Islam. This is by no means to argue that the nature of Islam or the history of the Arabs should be air-brushed in the name of political correctness. Indeed, it is critical that westerners as well as Muslims themselves come to have a better appreciation of these things. But essential sensitivities in this highly charged area must certainly be respected.

At the end of the day, however, the terror war will not be won without creating—and sustaining—new friends and allies of the United States throughout the Muslim world. And to do so, it is well to remember, will require political action, not just persuasive words.[8] This is a fundamental truth for all those interested in reviving and redefining the missions of public diplomacy today.

Notes

CHAPTER 1

1. Francis Fukuyama, "The End of History?" *The National Interest* (Summer 1989): 3–18. See further Fukuyama, *The End of History and the Last Man* (New York: The Free Press, 1992).

2. See especially United States Advisory Commission on Public Diplomacy, *Consolidation of USIA Into the State Department: An Assessment After One Year* (Washington, D.C., October 2000) (henceforth Advisory Commission Report); Stephen Johnson and Helle Dale, "How to Reinvigorate US Public Diplomacy," *Backgrounder* No. 1645 (Washington, D.C.: The Heritage Foundation, April 2003) (henceforth Heritage Foundation Report); Council on Foreign Relations Task Force, *Finding America's Voice: A Strategy for Reinvigorating U.S. Public Diplomacy* (New York: Council on Foreign Relations, 2003) (henceforth Council on Foreign Relations Report); Advisory Group on Public Diplomacy for the Arab and Muslim World, *Changing Minds, Winning Peace: A New Strategic Direction for U.S. Public Diplomacy in the Arab and Muslim World* (Washington, D.C., October 2003) (henceforth Advisory Group Report), *Report of the Defense Science Board Task Force on Strategic Communication* (Washington, D.C.: Department of Defense, September 2004) (henceforth Defense Science Board Report); and Public Diplomacy Council, *A Call for Action on Public Diplomacy* (Washington, D.C.: The Public Diplomacy Council, January 2005) (henceforth Public Diplomacy Council Report).

3. For a brief development of this argument, see Carnes Lord, "The Past and Future of Public Diplomacy," *Orbis* (Winter 1998): 49–72.

4. The only serious and informed discussion of this notion of which I am aware is Kim Cragin and Scott Gerwehr, *Dissuading Terror: Strategic Influence and the Struggle Against Terrorism* (Santa Monica, Cal.: RAND, 2005).

5. Proof in such matters is of course not possible; but consider at the anecdotal level the report of an interagency public diplomacy-related exercise in 2003 that had to be

terminated prematurely when it proved "dysfunctional." David E. Kaplan, "Hearts, Minds, and Dollars," *US News & World Report*, April 25, 2005, p. 24.

6. For a wide-ranging and thoughtful (if now dated) discussion, see Stuart J. D. Schwartzstein, ed., *The Information Revolution and National Security: Dimensions and Directions* (Washington, D.C.: Center for Strategic and International Studies, 1996).

7. Dwight D. Eisenhower, *The White House Years: Mandate for Change, 1953–1956* (Garden City, NY: Doubleday, 1963), p. 114.

8. Some speculations are offered in Carnes Lord, "In Defense of Public Diplomacy," *Commentary* (April 1984): 42–50.

9. A very relevant account is John J. Pitney, Jr., *The Art of Political Warfare* (Norman: University of Oklahoma Press, 2000).

CHAPTER 2

1. See the seminar article by Nye and Admiral William Owens, "The Information Edge," *Foreign Affairs* 75 (March/April 1996): 20–36.

2. For the British case see especially Niall Ferguson, *Empire: The Rise and Demise of the British World Order and the Lessons for Global Power* (London: Allen Lane, 2002).

3. See, for example, Stephen M. Walt, *Taming American Power* (New York: W.W. Norton, 2005).

4. Joseph S. Nye, Jr., *Soft Power: The Means to Success in World Politics* (New York: Public Affairs, 2004), esp. ch. 1.

5. *Ibid.*, pp. 2–5.

6. See notably William Riker, *The Art of Political Manipulation* (New Haven: Yale University Press, 1986) and *The Strategy of Rhetoric: Campaigning for the American Constitution* (New Haven: Yale University Press, 1996).

7. William E. Odom and Robert Dujarric, *America's Inadvertent Empire* (New Haven: Yale University Press, 2004).

8. Nye (*Soft Power*, pp. 69–72) reports polling results to this effect by the Pew Global Attitudes Project in four regions of the world in 2002, though oddly, without acknowledging this.

9. The global presence of CNN is well known, but few are aware that *Forbes, Foreign Affairs, Fortune*, the *Harvard Business Review, National Geographic, Newsweek*, and *Time* are all available in Japan in Japanese translation—an extreme but revealing case. Odom and Dujarric, *America's Inadvertent Empire*, p. 197.

10. Nye, *Soft Power*, p. 25.

11. *Ibid.*, p. 99.

12. For a detailed account, see Arch Puddington, *Broadcasting Freedom: The Cold War Triumph of Radio Free Europe and Radio Liberty* (Lexington: University Press of Kentucky, 2000), pp. 253–306.

13. The political scientist Harold Lasswell is perhaps the central figure here. See generally Christopher Simpson, *Science of Coercion: Communication Research and Psychological Warfare, 1945–1960* (New York: Oxford University Press, 1994).

14. See, for example, Derek Leebaert, *The Fifty-Year Wound: The True Price of America's Cold War Victory* (Boston: Little, Brown, 2002), ch. 10. For a recent attempt to assess the impact of Western broadcasting utilizing Soviet bloc archival material and oral history, see "Cold War Broadcasting Impact," Report on a

Conference Organized by the Hoover Institution and the Cold War International History Project of the Woodrow Wilson International Center for Scholars, Stanford University, October 2004.

15. For a compendium of views on the subject from this formative period, see *Public Diplomacy and the Future*, Hearings before the Subcommittee on International Operations of the Committee on International Relations, House of Representatives, 95th Cong., 1st Sess. (Washington, D.C.: USGPO, 1977). It would be wrong, however, to suppose that public diplomacy is an American invention; this honor must be awarded to the British. See notably Philip M. Taylor, *British Propaganda in the Twentieth Century: Selling Democracy* (Edinburgh: Edinburgh University Press, 1999).

16. See, for example, Richard H. Shultz and Roy Godson, *Dezinformatsiya: Active Measures in Soviet Strategy* (Washington, D.C.: Pergamon-Brassey's, 1984), Martin Ebon, *The Soviet Propaganda Machine* (New York: McGraw-Hill, 1987).

17. A certain amount of the resistance to public diplomacy within the current administration can be traced to officials concerned that public diplomacy is being used by others to "reverse engineer" policies that are unpopular within the Beltway (interviews with DoD and White House officials). Public diplomatists need to be especially sensitive to this bureaucratic trap.

18. For an analysis that focuses on the challenges posed by hostile exploitation of recent technological developments, especially the internet, see Timothy L. Thomas, *Cyber Silhouettes: Shadows Over Information Operations* (Fort Leavenworth, Kansas: Foreign Military Studies Office, 2005), a valuable work that focuses on Russia and China as well as Al-Qaeda.

19. See on this subject U.S. General Accounting Office, *U.S. International Broadcasting: Strategic Planning and Performance Management System Could be Improved* (Washington, D.C., September 2000), App. 2.

CHAPTER 3

1. See notably Robert Parry and Peter Kornbluh, "Iran-Contra's Untold Story," *Foreign Policy* 72 (Fall 1988): 3–30.

2. In fact, the Salvadoran FMLN ran sophisticated operations in the United States designed to influence public and particularly congressional opinion, including efforts to affect congressional elections. J. Michael Waller, *The Third Current of Revolution: Inside the 'North American Front' of El Salvador's Guerrilla War* (Lanham, Md.: University Press of America, 1991).

3. Robert Satloff, *The Battle of Ideas in the War on Terror: Essays on U.S. Public Diplomacy in the Middle East* (Washington, D.C.: The Washington Institute for Near East Policy, 2004), p. 68.

4. A classic treatment is Charles Frankel, *The Neglected Aspect of Foreign Affairs: American Educational and Cultural Policy Abroad* (Washington, D.C.: The Brookings Institution, 1965). See also Frank A. Ninkovich, *The Diplomacy of Ideas: U.S. Foreign Policy and Cultural Relations 1938–1950* (Cambridge: Cambridge University Press, 1981), Richard T. Arndt, *The First Resort of Kings: American Cultural Diplomacy in the Twentieth Century* (Washington, D.C.: Potomac Books, 2005).

5. The OSS in turn was modeled on the Political Warfare Executive, a clandestine British organization created by Winston Churchill.

6. The Air Force also has a PSYOP component, mainly in a technical support role. For a good sampling of recent PSYOP thinking in the U.S. military, see Frank L. Goldstein and Benjamin F. Finley, Jr., eds., *Psychological Operations: Principles and Case Studies* (Maxwell AFB, Ala.: Air University Press, 1996).

7. Mark Mazzetti and Borzou Daragahi, "U.S. Military Covertly Pays To Run Stories in Iraqi Press," *Los Angeles Times*, November 30, 2005. This article was followed by extensive coverage in virtually every major American newspaper.

8. Matt Kelley, "Pentagon Rolls Out Stealth PR," *USA Today*, December 14, 2005, Mark Mazzetti and Kevin Sack, "Planted PR Stories Not News to Military," *Los Angeles Times*, December 18, 2005.

9. As a National Security Council staff member with public diplomacy responsibilities at the time, I was personally aware of these otherwise little-known activities.

10. For the early history of American efforts in this field, see Lawrence C. Soley, *Radio Warfare: OSS and CIA Subversive Propaganda* (New York: Praeger, 1989). For the contemporary scene, see the website Clandestineradio.com.

11. J. Michael Waller, "Losing a Battle for Hearts and Minds," *Insight Magazine*, April 22, 2002.

12. A noteworthy example from the Reagan era is Evan Galbraith, who actively promoted administration policies such as the Strategic Defense Initiative during his tenure as ambassador to France: Evan G. Galbraith, *Ambassador in Paris: The Reagan Years* (Chicago: Regnery Gateway, 1987).

13. Kenneth A. Osgood, "Form before Substance: Eisenhower's Commitment to Psychological Warfare and Negotiations with the Enemy," *Diplomatic History* 24 (Summer 2000): 405–33, is an excellent account.

14. On this neglected subject see Raymond Cohen, *Theatre of Power: The Art of Diplomatic Signalling* (London: Longman, 1987). Beyond the role of presidents as such, however, there is an entire repertoire of symbolic or non-verbal communication by states that borders on if it is not simply an aspect of public diplomacy; this has rarely been systematically studied.

CHAPTER 4

1. Alison Jamieson, "The Italian Experience," in H. H. Tucker, ed., *Combating the Terrorists: Democratic Responses to Political Violence* (New York: Facts on File, 1988), pp. 122–47.

2. Patrick J. McDonnell, "Iraqi TV Targets Insurgents," *Los Angeles Times*, March 2, 2005.

3. In the fall of 2005, unmistakeable signs emerged of serious differences between the central Al Qaeda leadership and the self-proclaimed leading Al Qaeda operative in Iraq, Abu Musab al-Zarkawi: Bernard Haykel, "Terminal Debate," *New York Times*, October 11, 2005, Susan B.Glasser and Walter Pincus, "Seized Letter Outlines Al Qaeda Goals in Iraq," *Washington Post*, October 12, 2005. Little seems to have been done by Washington or U.S. forces in Iraq to capitalize on this development.

4. Andrea Stone, "In Poll, Islamic World Says Arabs Not Involved in 9/11," *USA Today*, February 27, 2002.

5. Exhaustively documented in Daniel Pipes, *The Hidden Hand: Middle East Fears of Conspiracy* (New York: St. Martin's, 1996), a book that has much relevance to the concerns of this study. It should be added that the phenomenon is not exclusively Arab—the Iranians in particular should be mentioned.

6. See Hugh Miles, *Al-Jazeera: The Inside Story of the Arab News Channel that is Challenging the West* (New York: Grove Press, 2005).

7. A report surfaced recently that President Bush raised with British Prime Minister Tony Blair at a meeting at the White House in April 2004 the possibility of an air strike against Al-Jazeera's headquarters in Doha, Qatar; if indeed true, it is not clear whether the president was joking. Kevin Sullivan and Walter Pincus, "Paper Says Bush Talked of Bombing Arab TV Network," *Washington Post*, November 23, 2005.

8. Fouad Ajami, "What the Muslim World is Watching," *New York Times Sunday Magazine*, November 18, 2001.

9. Much is complicated and unclear concerning the future U.S. military posture throughout the Middle East and Central Asia. It seems likely at a minimum that the United States will maintain a modest though significant ground presence in Afghanistan (anchored at Bagram Air Base) for the foreseeable future; in the Persian Gulf, assuming continuing progress in Iraq and stability elsewhere in the vicinity, it seems set to reassume within a few years what might be called an "offshore" presence—involving mainly naval and air forces—anchored in bases in Bahrain, Qatar, and the United Arab Emirates. Eric Schmitt, "Pentagon Construction Boom Beefs Up Mideast Air Bases," *New York Times*, September 18, 2005.

10. Between May and November 2005, according to one poll, the number of Pakistanis with a favorable opinion of the U.S. doubled from 23% to 46%, while unfavorable views declined from 48% to 28%; a February 2005 poll showed that fully 65% of Indonesians had a more favorable view of the U.S. than prior to the tsunami. Husan Haqqani and Kenneth Ballen, "Our Friends the Pakistanis," *Wall Street Journal*, December 19, 2005.

11. Pew Research Center for the People and the Press, May 2005; cited in Max Boot, "Our Extreme Makeover," *Los Angeles Times*, July 27, 2005.

12. Thomas L. Friedman, "Osama At the Kit Kat Club," *New York Times*, January 25, 2006, notes the recent unprecedented public criticism of bin Laden by spokesmen for the Egyptian Muslim Brotherhood, one of the original sources of Al-Qaeda's Islamist ideology.

13. See, for example, Grey E. Burkhart and Susan Older, *The Information Revolution in the Middle East and North Africa* (Santa Monica, CA: RAND Corporation, 2003); *Arab Reform Bulletin*, special issue on Arab Media and Reform (December 2004); Marc Lynch, "Arab Revolution Powered by Television," *Baltimore Sun*, March 6, 2005.

14. On Al-Arabiya see Samantha M. Shapiro, "The War Inside the Arab Newsroom," *New York Times*, January 2, 2005.

15. See particularly his speech at the American Enterprise Institute in Washington (*New York Times on the Web*, October 6, 2005).

16. Notably, by former national security adviser Zbigniew Brzezinski, "Do These Two Have Anything in Common?" *Washington Post*, December 4, 2005.

17. On this important issue see Stephen F. Hayes, "Down the Memory Hole: The Pentagon Sits on the Documents of the Saddam Hussein Regime," *The Weekly Standard*, December 19, 2005, Stephen F. Hayes, "Saddam's Terror Training Camps: What the Documents Captured From the Former Iraqi Regime Reveal—and Why They Should All Be Made Public," *The Weekly Standard*, January 16, 2006, Peter Hoekstra, "Needed: Arabic Translators," *Washington Times*, December 23, 2005.

18. There is some evidence that Israeli interest in the strategic influence instrument is increasing. See Amos Harel, "IDF Reviving Psychological Warfare Unit," *Ha'aretz*, January 25, 2005.

19. See, for example, Yossi Melman and Dan Raviv, *Friends in Deed: Inside the U.S.—Israel Alliance* (New York: Hyperion, 1994).

20. A place to start might be the fine study of Efraim Karsh and Inari Karsh, *Empires of the Sand: The Struggle for Mastery in the Middle East, 1789–1923* (Cambridge, Mass.: Harvard University Press, 1999), which convincingly challenges the conventional scholarly view (and the assumption of most Muslims today) that the Arabs were simply victimized by nineteenth century European imperialism. It calls welcome attention, among other things, to the egregious blunders of the Ottoman Turks, particularly in allying with the Central Powers in World War I.

21. Jeffrey N. Wasserstrom, "Asia's Textbook Case," *Foreign Policy* (January–February 2006): 80–82, reviewing *The Contemporary and Modern History of Three Asian Countries* (Beijing: Social Sciences Academic Press, 2005) (in Chinese). The countries involved were the People's Republic of China, Japan, and South Korea. Long-standing Chinese complaints about Japanese textbook accounts of World War II gave rise to this project and underline its potential political importance.

22. See notably Charles Krauthammer, "In Iran, Arming for Armageddon," *Washington Post*, December 16, 2005.

23. For a cogent plea along these lines, see Anthony H. Cordesman, "Beyond Anger and Counterterrorism: A New Grand Strategy for US and Arab Relations," unpublished paper, Center for Strategic and International Studies, September 13, 2004.

24. The extent to which the United States seems to view the parliamentary system as the default mode of democracy has been little remarked on, but is surely odd. Consider Carnes Lord, *The Modern Prince: What Leaders Need to Know Now* (New Haven: Yale University Press, 2003), ch. 8.

25. A promising initiative along these lines is the translation project "Library on Democracy" sponsored by the National Endowment for Democracy and directed by Ahmed al-Rahim.

26. See notably Dorrance Smith, "The Enemy On Our Airwaves," *Wall Street Journal*, April 25, 2005. The writer is a former newsman whose appointment as Assistant Secretary of Defense for Public Affairs was held up until very recently because of adverse reaction by some senators to this article.

27. See Steven R. Weisman, "Under Pressure, Qatar May Sell Al-Jazeera," *New York Times*, January 30, 2005.

28. Note that the Iraqi Governing Council did not share such qualms: Anthony Shadid, "Iraqi Council halts Arab TV Network's News Broadcasts," *Washington Times*, November 26, 2003.

29. According to one DoD official, jamming of Al-Jazeera was in fact considered, but a basic decision was made not to "try to structure the information environment."

30. For recent perspective on this crucial issue, see, for example, William Dalrymple, "Inside the Madrasas," *New York Review of Books*, December 1, 2005, pp. 16–20, Alexander Evans, "Understanding Madrasahs: How Threatening Are They?" *Foreign Affairs* (January/February 2006): 9–16, Steve Levine and Zahid Hussain, "Pakistan's Broad Education Ills," *Wall Street Journal*, August 19, 2005.

31. Note the strong indictment in the widely cited United Nations study, "Arab Human Development Report," p. 51

32. Paul Berman, *Terror and Liberalism* (New York: W.W. Norton, 2003), pp. 61–62.

33. For a recent assessment see, for example, Jackson Diehl, "In the Mideast, Democratic Momentum," *Washington Post*, December 19, 2005. A useful compendium of information on current developments in this area is *Democracy Digest*, the weekly bulletin of the Transatlantic Democracy Network (www.demdigest.net).

34. Henry Grunwald, in Council on Foreign Relations Report, p. 51.

35. In Germany, a translation of Michael Moore's *Stupid White Men* has sold over a million copies and was on the German best-seller list for more than 40 weeks in 2002 and 2003. Adam Garfinkle, "Anti-Americanism, U.S. Foreign Policy, and the War on Terrorism," in Adam Garfinkle, ed., *A Practical Guide to Winning the War on Terrorism* (Stanford, Cal.: Hoover Institution Press, 2004), ch. 16, is a good brief account; see also Jean-François Revel, *Anti-americanism*, trans. Diarmid Cammel (San Francisco: Encounter, 2003), Barry Rubin and Judith Colp Rubin, *Hating America: A History* (Oxford: Oxford University Press, 2004).

36. Robert Kagan, *Of Paradise and Power: America and Europe in the New World Order* (New York: Vintage Books, 2004), is a trenchant account.

37. Consider, however, the now well-known history of CIA clandestine support for *Encounter*, an anti-communist literary magazine geared to European intellectuals. See more generally Peter Coleman, *The Liberal Conspiracy: The Congress for Cultural Freedom and the Struggle for the Mind of Postwar Europe* (New York: The Free Press, 1989).

38. Little attention seems to have been given to China's deliberate transition in recent years from Soviet-style "propaganda" to American-style "public diplomacy," and the challenge this is already posing to American interests around the world. See, for example, Jane Perlez, "Chinese Move to Eclipse U.S. Appeal in South Asia," *New York Times*, November 18, 2004, Danna Harman, "China Eyes New Turf: S. America," *Christian Science Monitor*, November 19, 2004, Howard W. French, "Another Chinese Export is All the Rage: China's Language," *New York Times*, January 11, 2006.

39. Probably the most successful U.S. public diplomacy venture ever, in terms at least of sheer numbers, has been the so-called Special English program (simplified and pronounced clearly and slowly) broadcast to China by the Voice of America. A similar program might profitably be made available for Arabic speakers.

40. Steven Lee Myers, "Red Star Over Russian Airwaves: Military TV Network," *New York Times*, February 11, 2005; Alex Nicholson, "Satellite Channel to Repackage Russia," June 6, 2005, http://cnn.netscape.cnn.com/news/story.jsp?floc=FF-APO-1333%idq=/ff/story/0001%2F20050606%2F1143063933.htm%sc=1333.

41. See Philip Fiske de Gouveia, "Africa Needs an Al Jazeera," *Foreign Policy* (June 2005), www.foreignpolicy.com/story/cms.php?story_id=3115&print=1.

42. Hector Tobar, "Latin America Losing Faith in Democracy," *Los Angeles Times*, April 22, 2004.

43. See, for example, Roger Cohen, "An Obsession the World Doesn't Share," *New York Times*, December 5, 2004.

44. Private comment by a senior State Department official.

45. For an influential statement of this case see Niall Ferguson, *Colossus: The Price of America's Empire* (New York: Penguin Press, 2004). Ferguson, a British historian, actually welcomes an American empire, but questions whether Americans are capable of managing one. On his ideas see further Carnes Lord, "Dreams of Empire," *Claremont Review of Books* (Fall 2004): 11–12.

46. Materials for constructing such argumentation are readily available in books such as Michael Mandelbaum, *The Case for Goliath: How America Acts as the World's Government in the 21st Century* (New York: Public Affairs, 2005).

CHAPTER 5

1. For example, the *New York Times* reportedly withheld publication for a year of its recent story on warrantless NSA surveillance of terrorism-related communications involving one U.S. party.

2. For general discussion see Timothy E. Cook, *Governing with the News: The News Media as a Political Institution* (Chicago: University of Chicago Press, 1998), as well as Carnes Lord, *The Modern Prince*, pp. 185–89.

3. P.L. 94-350.

4. For a characteristic statement of what may be called the institutional VOA view of the Charter, see Alan L. Heil, Jr., *The Voice of America: A History* (New York: Columbia University Press, 2003), pp. 152–77.

5. Quoted in William Safire, "Equal Time for Hitler?" *New York Times*, September 20, 2001; see also Ellen Nakashima, "Broadcast with Afghan Leader Halted," *Washington Post*, September 23, 2001.

6. Consider Howard Kurtz, "CNN Chief Orders 'Balance' in War News," *Washington Post*, October 31, 2001; Bill Carter, "CNN, Amid Criticism in Israel, Adopts Terror Report Policy," *New York Times*, June 21, 2002.

7. Cited in Kenneth R. Timmerman, "The Other Air War," *Wall Street Journal*, November 9, 2001.

8. James Dao and Eric Schmitt, "A Nation Challenged: Hearts and Minds; Pentagon Readies Efforts to Sway Sentiment Abroad," *New York Times*, February 19, 2002.

9. See especially Franklin Foer, "Flacks Americana," *The New Republic*, May 20, 2002.

10. See Rowan Scarborough, "Rumsfeld Expresses Doubt on New Propaganda Office," *Washington Times*, February 25, 2002, "Rumsfeld Shuts Down Office Criticized for Propaganda Role," *Washington Times*, February 27, 2002, J. Michael Waller, "Losing a Battle for Hearts and Minds," *Insight Magazine*, April 22, 2002. Thomas E. Ricks, "Rumsfeld Kills Pentagon Propaganda Unit," *Washington Post*, February 27, 2002, quotes an unnamed military officer as saying that the new office was involved mainly in "defense marketing" (i.e. defense public diplomacy) and that only 5% of its planned work would have involved covert operations.

11. Interview with Simon P. Worden. See further Brig. Gen. Simon P. Worden, Lt. Col. Martin E. B. France, USAF, and Maj. Randall R. Correll, USAF (ret.), "Information War: Strategic Influence and the Global War on Terror," unpublished paper, October 2002.

12. Mark Mazzetti and Borzou Daragahi, "U.S. Military Covertly Pays to Run Stories in Iraqi Press," *Los Angeles Times*, November 30, 2005; see also Mark Mazzetti, "Covert Media Offensive In Iraq Sparks a Furor," *Los Angeles Times*, December 2, 2005.

13. For a cogent defense of these activities see Michael Schrage, "Use Every Article in the Arsenal: Good Press is a Legitimate Weapon," *Washington Post*, January 15, 2006.

14. Consider Carnes Lord, "Public Diplomacy: Past and Future," *Orbis* (Winter 1998): 49–72.

15. For a recent reprise of this theme, see Warren P. Strobel and Jonathan S. Landay, "State Dept. Program Excludes War Critics: Official Cites a Political 'Litmus Test' for Americans Selected to Speak Overseas," *Washington Post*, December 3, 2005.

16. John Micklethwait and Adrian Wooldridge, *The Right Nation: Conservative Power in America* (New York: Penguin, 2004).

CHAPTER 6

1. Clayton D. Laurie, *The Propaganda Warriors: America's Crusade Against Nazi Germany* (Lawrence, Kan.: University Press of Kansas, 1996).

2. On this history see especially Walter L. Hixson, *Parting the Curtain: Propaganda, Culture, and the Cold War, 1945–1961* (New York: St. Martin's Press, 1997), chs. 1–3, Wilson P. Dizard, Jr., *Inventing Public Diplomacy: The Story of the U.S. Information Agency* (Boulder, Colo.: Lynne Rienner, 2004), chs. 1–4.

3. Alfred H. Paddock, Jr., *U.S. Army Special Warfare: Its Origins* (Washington, D.C.: National Defense University Press, 1982).

4. Quoted in Hixson, *Parting the Curtain*, p. 19.

5. Dizard, *Inventing Public Diplomacy*, ch. 7.

6. Comprehensively listed in Lois W. Roth, "Public Diplomacy and the Past: The Search for an American Style of Propaganda (1952–1977)," *The Fletcher Forum* (Summer 1984): 353–96.

7. President Jimmy Carter, "Memorandum for Director, International Communications Agency," March 13, 1978 (text in Roth, "Public Diplomacy," pp. 389–91).

8. Panel on International Information, Education, and Cultural Relations, *International Information, Education, and Cultural Relations: Recommendations for the Future* (Washington, D.C.: Center for Strategic and International Studies, 1975).

9. Text in Christopher Simpson, *National Security Directives of the Reagan and Bush Administrations* (Boulder, Colo.: Westview, 1995), pp. 265–67.

10. A study carried out toward the end of the Reagan administration involving extensive interviewing of senior officials claims that "almost everyone consulted believes NSDD 77 has not worked." David I. Hitchcock, Jr., *US Public Diplomacy* (Washington, D.C.: Center for Strategic and International Studies, 1988), p. 22.

11. Presidential Decision Directive 68, "International Public Information" (April 1999). In an unusual arrangement, an interagency "secretariat" in support of this directive was established within the State Department's Office of Public Diplomacy and Public Affairs; this group proved reasonably active and effective, notably in the war against Serbia. For a brief account see Col. Brad Ward, "Strategic Influence Operations—The Information Connection" (Carlisle Barracks, Penna.: US Army War College, n.d.), pp. 9–11.

12. In the fall of 2001, the Joint Staff established an "Information Operations Resource Center" that was originally intended to serve as an interagency focus for strategic communications or influence operations in Afghanistan; other agencies declined to participate. A purely military successor, an "Information Operations Task Force," proved equally ineffective. See LTC Susan L. Gough, "The Evolution of Strategic Influence" (Carlisle Barracks, Penna.: US Army War College, n.d.), p. 32.

13. Karen DeYoung, "Bush Message Machine is Set to Roll With Its Own War Plan," *Washington Post*, March 19, 2003.

14. Interview with NSC official.

15. Daniel G. DuPont, "White House Reorganizes National Security Council Staff Structure," *Inside the Pentagon*, March 31, 2005.

16. Consider Walter Jajko, "It's Propaganda Time," *Los Angeles Times*, December 2, 2005. The writer is a retired Air Force brigadier general and former assistant to the Secretary of Defense for intelligence oversight.

17. For a general account see Abram N. Shulsky, *Silent Warfare: Understanding the World of Intelligence* (Washington: Brassey's, 1993).

18. Steven R. Weisman, "Rice to Group Foreign Aid In One Office In State Dept.," *New York Times*, January 19, 2006. State Department officials quoted in this article made a point of noting that the possibility is being left open of extending the coordinating role of the AID director (who would have a rank equivalent to the Deputy Secretary of State) to other cabinet agencies involved in foreign assistance, such as Agriculture or Health and Human Services.

CHAPTER 7

1. Quoted in Advisory Commission Report for 2000, p. 6.

2. On all this see particularly Heritage Foundation Report, as well as Carnes Lord, *The Presidency and the Management of National Security* (New York: The Free Press, 1988), pp. 46–52.

3. See, for example, Peter Carlson, "The U.S.A. Account," *Washington Post*, December 31, 2001, Stephen F. Hayes, "Uncle Sam's Makeover," *The Weekly Standard*, June 3, 2002, pp. 22–25.

4. Newt Gingrich, "Transforming the State Department," speech delivered at the American Enterprise Institute, Washington, D.C., April 22, 2003; "Rogue State Department," *Foreign Policy* (July–August 2003): 42–48. Of particular weight is the sweeping indictment of the State Department as a "crippled institution" in Hart-Rudman Commission, *Road Map for National Security: Imperative for Change* (Washington, D.C.: U.S. Commission for National Security/21st Century, 2001); see also Joel Mowbray, *Dangerous Diplomacy: How the State Department Threatens America's Security* (Washington, D.C.: Regnery, 2003), esp. chs. 5, 11. For an instructive survey and analysis of Foreign Service attitudes see Stephanie Smith Kinney, "Developing

Diplomats for 2010: If Not Now, When?" *American Diplomacy* (Summer 2000), available at www.unc.edu/depts/diplomat/AD_Issues/amdipl_16/kinney.

5. Interview with member of the U.S. Advisory Board for Public Diplomacy. Kinney (see last note) reports that many Foreign Service officers surveyed would like the Foreign Service to be more like the military in this and other respects.

6. In fact, I supported it conditionally in 1998: Lord, "The Past and Future of Public Diplomacy," pp. 70–71.

7. Of the major outside studies, only the Public Diplomacy Council Report calls for the reestablishment of USIA (which it renames the U.S. Public Diplomacy Agency), although a privatized entity comparable to USIA is recommended by the Council on Foreign Relations Report and the Defense Science Board Report. See also Leonard H. Marks, Charles Z. Wick, Bruce Gelb, and Henry E. Catto, "America Needs a Voice," *Washington Post*, February 26, 2005. (The writers are all former directors of USIA.)

8. There may be merit in the idea of establishing an independent, not-for-profit "Corporation for Public Diplomacy" along the lines of the Corporation for Public Broadcasting, as proposed by the Council on Foreign Relations Report, but not as a substitute for a robust Educational and Cultural Affairs bureau. In any event, the political carrying costs of such a move could well prove exorbitant.

9. Remarks of Under Secretary of State for Public Diplomacy and Public Affairs Karen Hughes at Town Hall for Public Diplomacy, Washington, D.C., September 8, 2005.

10. A planning unit was in fact created within IIP in September 2004, encompassing the public affairs as well as the public diplomacy function and tasked as the focal point of interagency coordination for the Under Secretary; a crisis response element is apparently another Karen Hughes initiative.

11. Little attention seems ever to have been given to this dimension of public diplomacy by the U.S. government. For a useful contrasting perspective see Mark Leonard, *Public Diplomacy* (London: The Foreign Policy Centre, 2002), especially ch. 3.

12. Reporting responsibilities for the Bureau of International Narcotics and Law Enforcement were only recently transferred from this Under Secretary to the Under Secretary for Political Affairs. Other recent developments in this area include the creation of a new Deputy Assistant Secretary of State for Democracy within the Bureau of Democracy, Human Rights, and Labor, creation of an outside Advisory Committee on democracy promotion, and a comprehensive internal review of U.S. democracy promotion strategies. See Office of the Spokesman, U.S. Department of State, Fact Sheet, July 29, 2005.

13. The logic of this arrangement, it should be noted, differs somewhat from the idea of public diplomacy as it existed in the days of USIA, as the "political action" component of traditional public diplomacy would migrate into the more diplomacy-oriented arena of democracy promotion and related issues.

14. Detailed discussion of public diplomacy field operations is beyond our scope, but one could imagine an arrangement whereby the PAOs and CAOs (Cultural Affairs Officers) in embassies would normally be from USIA, while IOs (Information Officers) would be supplied by State.

15. Allan M. Winkler, *The Politics of Propaganda: The Office of War Information 1942–1945* (New Haven: Yale University Press, 1978).

16. Interview with senior Senate staff member.

17. Defense Science Board Report, pp. 66–69. As noted earlier, the Council on Foreign Relations report similarly calls for a "Corporation for Public Diplomacy" on the model of the Corporation for Public Broadcasting.

CHAPTER 8

1. P.L. 103-236.

2. Radio/TV Marti, created in 1985 as a Cuban surrogate broadcasting entity, was formally part of VOA from its inception, an anomalous situation that was the result of a compromise in the prolonged fight in Congress over its authorizing legislation.

3. The language of the Act in this matter was artfully worded so as to suggest that such decisions are fundamentally technical in character. It is striking how infrequently this change has been challenged in recent studies of public diplomacy; consider, for example, the tentative and polite questioning of the Council on Foreign Relations Report, pp. 78–79.

4. Curiously, this occurred despite a change in the language of the BBG's mandate in the Foreign Affairs Reform and Restructuring Act (PL 105-277) of 1998 that excised the word "direct" from the key phrase "direct and supervise" of the older International Broadcasting Act. This legislation did, however, remove the BBG altogether from any control by USIA.

5. Pattiz has been little noticed in the national media, though see Neil King, Jr., "Sparking Debate, Radio Czar Retools Government Media," *Wall Street Journal*, June 20, 2005.

6. Radio Sawa was launched in March 2002, with four programming streams (reflecting differing regional tastes and interests) directed to Jordan, Egypt, Iraq, and the Persian Gulf; it will eventually broadcast to Palestine and seventeen countries in the Middle East and Africa. It uses a combination of FM, medium wave, short wave, digital audio satellite, and the internet, and broadcasts 24/7. Surveys indicate it is reaching as much as 50% of its target audience. See General Accounting Office, *US International Broadcasting: New Strategic Approach Focuses on Reaching Large Audiences but Lacks Measurable Program Objectives*, Report to the Committee on International Relations, US House of Representatives (July 2003).

7. Particularly hard-hit has been eastern Europe: VOA Estonian, Latvian, Lithuanian, Polish, Hungarian, Romanian, Bulgarian, Czech, Slovak, and Slovene were all completely abolished in early 2004.

8. Interviews with senior broadcasting officials.

9. Barbara Slavin, "VOA Changes Prompt Staffer Protests," *Washington Times*, July 13, 2004.

10. Interviews with senior broadcasting officials.

11. The "Freedom Promotion Act" of 2002 (HR 3969), sponsored principally by Rep. Henry Hyde (R-Ill.), proposed among other things to amend the International Broadcasting Act to reorganize broadcasting under a new U.S. International Broadcasting Agency; the bill passed the House but died in the Senate.

12. Robert Novak, "Biden Playing Politics," www.cnn.com/2005/POLITICS/ 06/23/biden.politics. According to Novak, Pattiz contributed $360,000 to the Democratic Party in the 2000 election cycle. Also important for understanding the dynamics of the situation is the fact that influential BBG member Ted Kaufman is a

former chief of staff and close friend of Senator Biden. In January 2006, Pattiz announced his resignation from the BBG.

13. Interviews with senior broadcasting officials.

14. A survey of senior program managers at the radios has shown that a majority support significant reduction in overlap between language services; most thought overlap should occur in only a few countries or none at all. General Accounting Office, *U.S. International Broadcasting*, p. 24.

15. A move to merge RFE with VOA in 1993 was killed in the Senate Foreign Relations Committee.

16. The Board would therefore represent only the private sector, not the State Department or any other government agency. It would also be advisable to take steps, formal or informal, to ensure that a new Board is truly representative of the relevant private sector and not simply of the broadcasting industry or the journalism profession.

17. An alternative vision, said to have some support in the Senate, would be to subordinate VOA unambiguously to the State Department and transform it into a kind of global C-SPAN. I believe direct subordination to the State Department is unworkable as long as VOA is producing its own news; but without a news operation, the appeal of such a station to the rest of the world would have to be extremely limited.

CHAPTER 9

1. DoD definitions of the term show significant variation; some include "international broadcasting" as well as "information operations."

2. Information Operations as currently defined are "the integrated employment of the core capabilities of electronic warfare, computer network operations, psychological operations, military deception and operational security, in concert with specified supporting and related activities, to influence, disrupt, corrupt or usurp adversarial human and automated decision making while protecting our own." IO falls within the purview of the U.S. Strategic Command, but PSYOP capabilities belong to the U.S. Special Operations Command—an awkward situation whose complications have not yet been fully worked out. See further Leigh Armistead, ed., *Information Operations: Warfare and the Hard Reality of Soft Power* (Washington, D.C.: Brassey's, 2004).

3. Very recently, "international defense information" has gained some currency at senior levels in the Pentagon as an umbrella term for public affairs and defense public diplomacy.

4. Joint Pubs 1-02, *Department of Defense Dictionary of Military and Associated Terms* (Washington, D.C.: US Government Printing Office, 1994).

5. Criticizing recent developments in Iraq, for example, a "senior defense official" reportedly commented: "The movement of information has gone from the public affairs world to the psychological operations world. What's at stake is the credibility of people in uniform." Mark Mazzetti, "PR Meets Psy-Ops in War on Terror," *Los Angeles Times*, December 1, 2004.

6. Interviews with DoD officials and former PSYOP officers.

7. Interviews with DoD officials.

8. Interviews with DoD and White House officials.

9. It should be added that the grounds for this distrust are not uniform; some are merely skeptical of the sophistication and effectiveness of military PSYOP efforts.

10. For Afghanistan, see, for example, Bradley Graham, "U.S. Beams Its Message to Afghans," *Washington Post*, October 19, 2001, Greg Jaffe, "Elite Army Psychological Unit Aims a Propaganda Campaign at Afghans," *Wall Street Journal*, November 8, 2001, Philip Smucker, "The U.S. Army's Men in Black . . . Turbans," *Christian Science Monitor*, May 30, 2002, Levon Sevunts, "Talk is New Weapon in War Against Insurgency," *Washington Times*, June 7, 2005. For Iraq: Walter Pincus, "U.S. Plans Appeal to Iraqi Officers," *Washington Post*, September 30, 2002, Greg Jaffe and Carla Anne Robbins, "U.S. Is Placing Materiel in Gulf, Opens Iraqi Psychological Drive," *Wall Street Journal*, October 4, 2002, Michael Elliott and Massimo Calabresi, "Inside the Secret Campaign to Topple Saddam," *Time*, December 2, 2002, Ann Scott Tyson, "Hearts, Minds, Leaflets: War's Psychological Side," *Christian Science Monitor*, January 30, 2003, Thom Shanker and Eric Schmitt, "Firing Leaflets and Electrons, U.S. Wages Information War," *New York Times*, February 24, 2003, Vernon Loeb, "With Leaflets and Broadcasts, U.S. Aims to Sway Iraqi Minds," *Washington Post*, March 17, 2003, Andrew Koch, "'Hearts and Minds' Key to U.S. Iraq Strategy," *Jane's Defense Weekly*, March 19, 2003, Vernon Loeb, "Psychological Operations Go Into High Gear," *Washington Post*, March 21, 2003, James Dao, "Trying to Win Iraqi Hearts and Minds on the Battlefield," *New York Times*, April 6, 2003, Andrew Koch, "Information War Played Major Role in Iraq," *Jane's Defense Weekly*, July 23, 2003.

11. Christopher J. Lamb, *Review of Psychological Operations Lessons Learned from Recent Operational Experience* (Washington, D.C.: National Defense University Press, September 2005). The study was commissioned by Deputy Under Secretary of Defense for Policy Ryan Henry.

12. *Department of Defense Information Operations Roadmap*, October 2003, as quoted in Lamb, p. 26. This classified document does not recognize "strategic psychological operations" as a military mission, a position endorsed also (p. 9) by Lamb.

13. Lamb, p. 41; for the four mission areas, see p. 9.

14. An exception is Robin A. Campbell, Lt Col Annette N. Foster, ANG, and LTC Steven J. Smith, USA, "Harnessing the Military's Voice: An Argument for a Greater Role in Public Diplomacy by the U.S. Military," National Security Program Discussion Paper, John F. Kennedy School of Government, Harvard University, 2005.

15. The term "international military information" gained some currency during the Clinton administration principally as a euphemism for PSYOP, but seems to have fallen into disuse. On its origin, see Campbell, Foster and Smith, n. 25.

16. Pentagon officials involved with strategic communications are acutely aware of DoD's multiple failures to deal effectively in a public relations sense with the legal and policy issues concerning interrogations and related matters at Guantanamo Bay and of course at Abu Ghraib prison in Baghdad.

17. As proposed by Campbell, Fisher, and Smith, pp. 35–39. One of the problems PSYOP has long encountered in gaining understanding and acceptance within the military is its virtual monopoly by the Army. It would be of particular importance to create viable communities of strategic communicators in the Navy and Marine Corps.

See CDR Randall G. Bowdish, USN, "Psychological Operations...From the Sea," *Proceedings* (February 1998): 70–72.

18. This would in effect replace or absorb the recently established Joint Strategic PSYOP Element, currently co-located with the headquarters of USSOCOM at MacDill Air Force Base in Florida.

19. This would also make good sense in light of the proximity of JFCOM to Washington (it is based in Norfolk, Virginia)—a major limitation of USSOCOM. It would be very important to have such a command located in the immediate Washington area, for example, at Fort Belvoir or Andrews Air Force Base. "Strategic Communication" as I understand it would not be a component of "Information Operations" and would have no relationship to USSTRATCOM except perhaps as a source of technical support.

20. Maj. Don Langley, USAF, "New 'JPASE' Sets the Pace for Joint Military Public Affairs," draft paper, JFCOM, January 18, 2006.

21. Alternatively, there could be a single multi-agency public diplomacy institute. As a practical matter, however, someone has to be in charge of such an organization, and DoD has the great advantage of readier access to large amounts of federal dollars.

22. Notably, by eliminating a policy role in this area for the office of the Assistant Secretary of Defense for Special Operations and Low Intensity Conflict, which is currently responsible for the PSYOP portfolio.

23. A final point: there is also an argument for removing PSYOP even in the narrow sense I have redefined it here from the special operations world, given the low priority and lack of real understanding that it tends to encounter there as well as its ghettoization relative to conventional forces. Perhaps a case could be made for transferring the Army civil affairs/PSYOP command to JFCOM as well.

24. For a general discussion see Tony Corn, *The Influence of Soft Power Upon History: U.S. Military Soft Power from Alfred Mahan to Joseph Nye* (forthcoming 2006).

25. See Timothy C. Shea, "Transforming Military Diplomacy," *Joint Force Quarterly* (3rd Quarter 2005): 49–52.

CHAPTER 10

1. On the general question of the National Security Council staff and interagency system see Carnes Lord, *The Presidency and the Management of National Security* (New York: The Free Press, 1988).

2. The mostly sensible Heritage Foundation Report argues that OGC should have this role; but it is unrealistic and inappropriate for an entity completely outside the NSC system to have such a coordinating role, given the inescapably close connection between public diplomacy and policy.

3. Defense Science Board Report, p. 65; Council on Foreign Relations Report, pp. 31–34. The language of the latter report is ambiguous on the issue of operational authority, a highly contentious issue.

4. Advisory Group Report, pp. 59–60. This figure would also be supported by a "President's Public Diplomacy Experts Board," analogous to the President's Foreign Intelligence Advisory Board but including the under secretaries of state and defense—a wholly unworkable notion.

5. This solution is proposed by Ambassador Diana Dougan, former White House staffer and Assistant Secretary of State for International Communications and Information Policy, and a member of the Djerijian Commission. She calls the proposed agency "The Office of United States Public Diplomacy, Education and Exchange." "Re-organizing Public Diplomacy: A Different Viewpoint" (unpublished paper, 2003).

6. Consider, for example, the generally ineffective performance of White House "drug czars" (directors of the Office of National Drug Control Policy) and science advisers (directors of the Office of Science and Technology Policy).

7. Ambassador Dougan takes a step in this direction in suggesting that the Under Secretary of State for Public Affairs and Public Diplomacy might also serve as head of the new agency on an interim basis until appropriate legislation and resource allocations can be put in place.

8. It should be noted that the phrase "White House" can have a variety of meanings in this context. There are important differences in the perceived bureaucratic clout of offices within the Executive Office of the President, depending on whether they are located literally in the White House, in the Old Executive Office Building (directly adjacent to the White House), or the New Executive Office Building (a block away on 17th Street). USTR occupies the latter; it is probably the appropriate home for a public diplomacy entity of the sort we are describing.

9. It is important to be clear, however, that I am not suggesting that this entity should have responsibilities for economic or development assistance or for stability and reconstruction operations in the aftermath of military action. But it bears some similarity to the "Agency for Stability Operations" recently proposed in a study by the Center for Strategic and International Studies, *Beyond Goldwater-Nichols: Defense Reform for a New Strategic Era*, Phase 1 Report (Washington, D.C., March 2004), pp. 64–65.

10. Lamb, *Review of Psychological Operations Lessons Learned*, pp. 20–21; this judicious discussion has considerable relevance for public diplomacy generally.

11. Interviews with State Department official and Senate senior staff member.

12. For a good brief discussion see Mark Leonard, *Public Diplomacy* (London: The Foreign Policy Centre, 2002), ch. 4. See also Carnes Lord, "Crisis Management: A Primer," *IASPS Research Papers in Strategy*, No. 7 (Washington/Jerusalem: Institute for Advanced Strategic and Political Studies, 1998).

13. This co-chairing arrangement is vital, it can be argued, to underline the extent to which these missions transcend traditional diplomacy and centrally involve an array of agencies other than the State Department—and also to encourage State to take a greater lead in this area than has been the case in the past.

CHAPTER 11

1. The U.S.-U.K. Coalition Information Centers that operated for a period after 9/11 are exceptional in this regard. It would be interesting to know more about their actual functioning.

2. Leonard, *Public Diplomacy*, esp. ch. 3.

3. *Ibid.*, pp. 48–49. It might also be mentioned that even the British Broadcasting Corporation has not always been supportive of recent U.S. policy in the Middle East.

See, for example, Josh Chafetz, "The Disgrace of the BBC: Unfair, Unbalanced, and Afraid," *The Weekly Standard*, August 25, 2003.

4. Consider the interesting case of Norwegian "niche diplomacy" (Leonard, *Public Diplomacy*, app. II).

5. In his unpublished paper on the history of the Office of Strategic Influence, Worden claims that the most important function of this organization was actually to focus a "joint planning progress" across agencies and coalition partners.

6. A promising start in this area is the recently formed Business for Diplomatic Action, an association of business leaders with communications-related expertise and international experience.

7. The recent "Kingdom of Heaven," an incoherent, wildly ahistorical farrago of political correctness, is a good object lesson. One can also question whether Stephen Spielberg was entirely responsible in devoting an entire film to Israeli assassination operations against the Palestinian Black September group.

8. An effective statement of this case is Robert Satloff, "Tapping America's Anti-Islamist Allies across the Muslim World," in Garfinkle, ed., *A Practical Guide to Winning the War on Terrorism*, ch. 15. See also more generally Defense Science Board Report, ch. 3.

Index